More by David Dye

Winning Well:

A Manager's Guide to Getting Results Without Losing Your Soul
Your complete guide to transform results with quick practical action—complete with examples, stories, and online assessments.

Glowstone Peak

Join Selvia on a journey of influence, courage, and hope. A leadership themed picture book perfect for readers of all ages.

The
SEVEN THINGS
Your Team Needs to Hear You Say

The
SEVEN
THINGS
Your Team Needs
to Hear You Say

LEAD PRODUCTIVE, ENERGIZED, AND INNOVATIVE TEAMS TODAY

DAVID M. DYE

Requests for permission to make copies of any part of the work should be submitted to Let's Grow Leaders at 303 S. Broadway Ste 200-332, Denver, CO 80209 or 1.800.972.5082.

Publisher Info:
Let's Grow Leaders
303 S. Broadway Ste 200-332
Denver, CO 80209

Cover and book design: John Sellards
Editor: Alexandra O'Connell

www.LetsGrowLeaders.com

Printed in the United States of America
First printing: October 2013
Second printing: October 2018

ISBN: 978-0-9898581-0-6

*To my sisters and brother, who tolerated all the times
I got it wrong and loved me anyway.*

Thank you.

Contents

Introduction

If you're looking for a deep discussion of leadership theory, this book is not for you. You can walk into any bookstore or online merchant and find a large selection of those books, but if you're like most frontline team leaders, midlevel managers, small business owners, and supervisors, you don't have time for that.

You need help now.

You have one thousand things to do and only have time for twenty – if you skip lunch. You need tools you can use immediately to build a motivated, engaged, productive team and you need them in clear language.

And (if I may be so bold) the last thing you need is another debate about the difference between leaders and managers. If you're a supervisor in the 21st century and you want to succeed, you must lead *and* manage.

I once spoke with John G. Miller, the author of *The Question Behind the Question*, and he told me the highest compliment anyone could ever pay him was to say that his writing was practical.

In Miller's spirit, I hope to have provided you a resource that you will find practical, a book you can return to time and time again as you add these tools to your leadership repertoire. Beyond practicality, however, I also hope to encourage you...because you are needed.

Your team needs you to lead. *We* need you to lead. Philosophy and theory have a place, but there comes a time when, as Voltaire said, "We must cultivate our garden," stop discussing philosophy, and get things done.

Your team is waiting. Will you say what they need to hear?

Part One:
The Slow Road to
Frustration and Failure

Chapter 1
What to Do?

"What the heck would you do in a situation like that?"

~ Napoleon Dynamite

DO YOU REMEMBER the first team you ever led?

I'll never forget mine...

I was sitting at the kitchen table eating a bowl of Honey Nut Cheerios. At 11 years old, I was the oldest of six children. It was a warm Saturday in May, my mother was at work, and my father was running late. As he rushed through the kitchen on his way out the door, he stopped, pointed his finger in a sweep that took in the whole house, and said in a stern voice:

"David, this house is filthy. I want it spotless by the time I get home. You're in charge. Now get it done and I'll see you tonight."

He didn't say "or else..." but I understood this to be a serious matter.[1]

---

1 Understand that those were different times. Today in the United States you would not leave an 11 year old to care for five brothers and sisters. When I was a child, it was not unusual – especially for working class families.

I sat there, spoon in hand, and asked myself questions that will sound familiar to every new leader:

What now?
How can I get everyone to do what has to be done?
What will happen if I don't get it done?
Why me?

I pondered these questions for several minutes and then…
Inspiration.
In a blinding flash of insight, I had it!
"CheriMaryEstherDannyRachael!" I hollered (it was an accomplishment to name everybody in one breath). "C'mon…everyone go downstairs. We've got to clean the house. Dad said so."

To this day, I'm amazed that it worked: everyone trooped down to the basement. Everyone, that is, but me. Once everyone was downstairs, I climbed the stairs and…

I locked the door.

An interior door separated the stairs leading down to the basement from the rest of the house. I called down to my siblings, "I've locked the door – you can come out as soon as the basement is clean!"

Yes, that's right.

My earliest leadership memory is of locking my younger brothers and sisters in the basement.

Unfortunately, it would not be the last time I relied on fear, power, and control to motivate a team (hey – I was only 11. I thought it was brilliant at the time!). You can imagine what our family gatherings are like. I do get teased about those days, but fortunately, they've forgiven me my early leadership mistakes…I hope!

The fact is, the leadership model I used when at 11 may work in the short-term, but in the longer-term can lead to frustration, disengagement, and failure. Part One of this book will focus on fear, how fear manifests in the workplace, and introduce tools you can use to build a strong, dynamic team.

In Part Two, you will meet many leaders who found themselves in a variety of circumstances far more challenging than an 11 year old cleaning the house. You'll meet Walt, who was made President of a Fortune 500 company just as its stock had lost 95 percent of its value. You'll meet Christine, who was asked to build a business from scratch – in prison. And you'll meet Rick, who found himself in charge of a large urban high school with no notice, no computers, and facing a student walkout.

These leaders, and the others you'll meet in this book, have very different stories, but they share three things in common: who they were as people, what they said, and how they treated their teams. Actually, they share a fourth thing in common – they all succeeded in leading their organizations with motivated, engaged, and productive teams.

I hope you benefit from their stories as much as I have.

In Part Three, we will look at how to put these phrases into practice, overcome barriers to change, and transform your influence!

As a reader of *The Seven Things Your Team Needs to Hear You Say* you will want to reflect and apply these tools to your own leadership. I have prepared a complimentary downloadable workbook full of reflection questions and exercies you can use as you read. Go to https://letsgrowleaders.com/downloadable-resources/ right now and download your free copy of the workbook so you can have it in your hands before you turn another page. Go ahead, I'll wait...

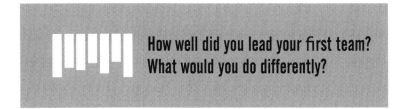

How well did you lead your first team? What would you do differently?

Chapter 2
How We React to Fear

"Only when we are no longer afraid do we begin to live."

-Dorothy Thompson, Journalist

BEFORE WE GO any farther, I'd like to do a little thought experiment with you. I will describe a scenario and I want you to picture yourself in the situation as specifically as you can. After reading the scenario, close your eyes if you need to and think about how you would really respond.

Are you ready?

Good!

Now, imagine yourself in a parking lot.

It's dark – well after sunset. Maybe you're leaving late from work or you're just getting back to your car after a late night with friends. Your car is the only one left in the parking lot. A streetlight shines in the distance, but otherwise it is dark and you are all alone – you can't see anyone else.

As you approach the car and pull your keys out of your pocket or purse, you hear footsteps. They're coming from behind you, but you resist the urge to glance over your shoulder. Maybe you don't want to attract attention or look foolish.

Unfortunately, as you near your car, the footsteps come closer and a man's voice says, "Don't move. Give me all your money."

In the moment his words settle in, you feel the barrel of a gun pressed against your back.

Now, what do you do?

Picture your reaction and emotions very carefully, with as much detail as you can. Maybe you've actually experienced being robbed at gunpoint. If so, remember how you actually responded.

- What do you do?
- What emotions do you experience?
- What do you *wish* you could do?

WHAT DID YOU DO?

Whenever I do this exercise with live audiences, the responses cluster in a few categories. See if what you did fits into one of these groups:

Creative Escape

These are the people who say, "I would fake a heart attack or pretend to faint and hope it scares him enough that he leaves me alone."

Fight Back

In larger audiences there are usually one or two individuals who have special training. I've met martial artists, military veterans, and state patrol officers who said they would fight back, incapacitate, and disarm the robber.

Negotiate

This is a rare response. These are the people who imagine they would bargain with the robber. Sometimes they are motivated by compassion (e.g., "You don't have to do this. Let's talk about it.").

Run

These folks just run. Some get creative (I'd dive over the car and then run!).

Hand It Over

These people (and I am one of them!) say something like, "I'd hand over my wallet or purse," or "I'd put my hands up and tell him, 'My wallet's in my back pocket.'" This is far and away the most common response. Eighty percent or more of most audiences say they would give the robber the money he asked for.[2]

A PREDICTION

As many times as I've taken people through this scenario, there is one response I have never heard and I will guarantee that you didn't think about it either:

You did not reach into your pocket, pull out your smartphone, contact your bank, cash out all your retirement savings, sell your house, sell your car, and then send it to the robber.

Of course not – it's ludicrous. Outrageous! Who would do such a thing? I don't know anyone who would. Do you?

Think about this for a moment. Despite a loaded gun being pressed against your back and the robber explicitly telling you to give him *all your money*, you did not give it all. Not remotely.

No one else would either.

If you're like most people, you gave him ten or twenty dollars, maybe more if you carry lots of cash. That's it. Despite threatening your life –

---

2 When confronted by an armed robber, law enforcement officials recommend handing over your cash. Money can be replaced, you cannot.

your most precious resource, the thing we cherish and hold dearer than almost anything else – all he got was a few lousy dollars.

Why?

Because when we're scared, we do the least amount possible to get out of the situation.

Consider your emotions while you imagined being robbed. Most people report a strong mix of anger and fear. For some, the anger produces a desire to fight back until they realize the robber's gun gives him too much power. For others, the fear is nearly overwhelming (I've had participants proclaim in front of their friends, "I would wet myself and then give him my money!"), and some report that they can barely move.

When confronted at gunpoint, most people experience a common set of emotions we know as "fight or flight" – the overwhelming desire to protect ourselves by attacking or running away.

The gun makes fighting back a dangerous proposition. Without special training, you're at an extreme disadvantage when facing a loaded gun.

So fighting back is out and we are left with one option: give the robber what he wants. Even then, we only give the least amount needed to escape the situation (the cash in our pocket).

 When people are scared, they will either: Fight back or do the minimum necessary to escape the situation.

Chapter 3
Fear in the Workplace

"I have never seen an outstanding organization where employees do not feel valued."

~Karen Martin, Author, The Outstanding Organization

FEAR AND LEADERSHIP

Let's leave our robber behind and get back to your team. As a leader, when you use fear to motivate, you are effectively asking your team to give *their very least effort* or, worse still, to fight back.

This has nothing to do with who you've hired, how mature they are, which generation they come from, or how well you've trained them. It has everything to do with the fact that they are people and that people react in known and predictable ways when they are scared. When they're threatened at gunpoint, people want to fight back or escape. Most don't fight back because of the unbalanced power equation. So they do the least possible to escape by surrendering the few dollars they have on them.

When you use fear to motivate (as I did with my brothers and sisters) you produce the same fight or flight reactions in your team. It's not their fault and they're not bad people – it's just human nature.

On a business team, fight or flight can take different forms.

FIGHT

First, let's look at "fight." When employees react to fear with anger and the desire to fight back, it may look like:

- Physical confrontation
- Inappropriate verbal arguments
- Sabotage
- Undermining
- Gossip and "whisper" campaigns
- Hyper-politics (focused on power, not productivity)

There are many ways for employees to fight. Some of them are obvious, but others are passive-aggressive and more difficult to detect. Clearly, any time your team members act from fear-motivated anger, it's unhealthy and can destroy your team and eventually your organization.

FLIGHT

Remember the robber's gun?

It placed him in such a position of power that fighting back would be useless for most of us. Now, you may be thinking, "Wait a minute. I'm a nice person, I don't have a gun pointed at my team!"

However, if you're in a business environment, your position as a team leader or supervisor may very well give you a similar "gun" that is always pointed at your people: the ability to terminate employment.

Even with due process and human resource guidelines meant to prevent supervisor abuses and protect employees, your ability to take away a person's income and livelihood is a very real threat *to them*, even if you never abuse your position.

This isn't about you.

As I write this, unemployment remains persistently high and may be worse than the reported numbers due to people who have given up looking for work or are underemployed. These conditions have a very real impact on how secure people feel about their employment.

In addition to environmental insecurity, personal experiences can introduce additional fear. You certainly know someone who has had, or have personally experienced, the boss who could work the system and get someone fired or just make life so miserable with reduced hours or degrading work that the employee felt they had to quit. [3]

You may not be that kind of supervisor (I sure hope not!), but regardless of who you are, these are the emotional realities much of your workforce brings to the team *before you have said a word*. As a result, whether you actively use the threat of termination or not, many of your team already feel that particular gun pointed at them.

The consequence of that employment-gun is just the same as the robber's physical gun: it unbalances the power equation and makes it far less likely that your employees would fight back and far more likely they will "flee." Now, I don't mean flee as in "run out the door screaming in terror." Remember that when people are scared and don't have power to fight back, **they do the least possible to get out of the situation**.

I'm sure you know what it looks like when staff give their least, but let's take a closer look – starting with you. When teams act from fear, you don't get the results you expect; your team doesn't problem solve, they wait for you to solve problems, make decisions, and come up with new ideas; no one takes responsibility; people seem lifeless; as a

---

3 For the supervisors who use these tactics: I understand your frustration. Sometimes the system can seem to protect people who aren't doing what they're supposed to do. Chapter Ten is for you. In the meantime, know that using these passive-aggressive tactics undermines your credibility, decreases your influence, and gets you the opposite of what you want in the long run: a healthy, high performance team.

leader, you find yourself frustrated, snapping at people, and saying
things like:

- "No one will do anything unless I yell!"
- "Why doesn't anyone else around here care?"
- "Why don't they get it?"
- "Do I have to do everything myself?"

It's an insidious trap – the more you use fear, the less people will do
and the more you feel like you have to use fear to get anything done at
all. The very tool you're using to motivate your team makes it more and
more difficult to get the results you want. Your stress skyrockets, you feel
isolated, alone, and eventually this will impact your physical health and
relationships outside of work. You are on the slow road to leadership
frustration and failure.

Now let's take a look at what your team members are saying. During
an informal survey in the fall of 2012, I had the opportunity to speak
with team members throughout many organizations and industries including healthcare, technology, waste management, and human service
and (in just 10 days!) I heard the following:

- "I've quit caring."
- "I've just stopped trying."
- "Why bother?"
- "I give up."
- "Just go along to get along."
- "When someone bothers to tell me what to do, then we'll
  worry about it."
- "What's the point?"
- "It doesn't matter what you do."
- "They don't care, so why should I?"

- "All their statements from the stage don't mean anything."

Not a pretty picture, is it? These folks were discouraged, depressed, and disengaged.

Now, not every one of these statements results from supervisors using fear – some were the result of several bad management practices and one or two included disgruntled employees who were not taking responsibility for their own situation. However, in doing the background work, what I found most sad was that some of the people making these comments were previously top performers in their organization and in every single case, managers and supervisors relied on fear. Talk about lost potential!

Together, these comments give you a good picture of what it looks like when employees give their least. I'm sure if you knew your team was talking and acting like this, you'd be frustrated. The thing is, you're not going to hear it. They'll think it, they'll feel it, and they'll act accordingly, give you their minimum effort – but unless you're lucky, very few will have the courage to tell you that you're undermining your own productivity.[4]

But while they may not tell *you*, they *will* tell someone. Here are just a few statistics from recent employee studies:

- 65 percent of employees say they would choose a better boss over a pay raise.[5]
- 71 percent of American workers aren't engaged or are actively disengaged from their work.[6]
- Barely one in five employees (21 percent) are engaged on the job. [7]

---

4 For more on making criticism work for you, check out my article at: https://letsgrowleaders.com/2017/12/14/6-ways-to-get-the-information-you-need-to-make-the-best-decisions/
5 PRWEB. "Two-Thirds of America Unhappy at Job." October 16, 2012. http://www.prweb.com/releases/2012/10/prweb10013402.htm. Accessed November 1, 2012.
6 Gallup. "Majority of American Workers Not Engaged in Their Jobs." October 28, 2011. Nikki Blacksmith and Jim Harter. http://www.gallup.com/poll/150383/Majority-American-Workers-Not-Engaged-Jobs.aspx. Accessed November 1, 2012.
7 Towers Watson. 2012 Global Workforce Study: Engagement at Risk – Driving Strong Performance In a Volatile Global Environment. http://towerswatson.com/assets/pdf/2012-Towers-Watson-Global-Workforce-Study.pdf. Accessed November 15, 2012.

These are amazing statistics, and come from a variety of sources.

Only one in five people are engaged in their work? Think about what that means in terms of lost productivity, lost customers, and lost impact. It's huge!

IS IT ME?

I'm sure by now you recognize the negative consequences of using fear to motivate a team:

- It gets the least effort from your people, or
- People may fight back with politics, sabotage, or undermining, and
- It traps you in a vicious cycle where the more you use it, the more you feel you have to use it.

In my work with leaders, they frequently say something like, "I get it, fear doesn't work, but I don't lead like that. Who are these fear-based managers?"

It's a question I hear regularly.

It's a question I even asked myself...until one day during my first year as a department leader, when I had a conversation with Mikayla, an employee who nearly trembled as she sat down to talk with me. When she finally composed herself, her opening words were, "David, I know you're about to fire me and I just wanted to – "

What?!

I never knew her performance to be anything but wonderful. I had no intention of firing her. In fact, she had a reputation for going above and beyond and frequently assisting other teams in her area of expertise.

As we discussed the situation, it became clear to me that her direct manager had not learned how to communicate or take personal responsibility for his influence. Anytime he was frustrated, he told his team that I was upset and they had better get things done "or else."

This was a huge leadership wake-up call for me. Clearly, I needed to take responsibility for my midlevel managers and make sure they had the tools to lead effectively and were using them. It also showed me that despite my best intentions, fear was a reality for some of my team members.

That was my responsibility; it started with me. I had set expectations for a manager who didn't know what to do, was inadequately trained, was afraid to let me down, and so resorted to fear to motivate his team.

I wasn't intentionally using fear as a motivational tool, but there it was – a stark reality for Mikayla.

Or maybe you can identify with one of my coaching clients, Kimberly. She manages a clothing store and entered into her management role with great intentions. Here is her story in her own words:

> "When I started as a manager, everything was great. I resolved to be supportive, encouraging, and serve my team. For a couple months we did great, but then I got the report for my first quarterly sales figures…and I fell apart. I snapped at my younger staff, was passive aggressive with my senior staff, who I thought should know better, and finally had to take myself off the sales floor because I thought I was doing more harm than good. I was so frustrated – in just one day I lost all my good intentions."

Kimberly switched over to fear, power, and control when faced with the stress of not producing the results that were her responsibility. She's not alone – nearly half of surveyed workers say that in times of stress their boss does not stay calm and in control.[8]

---

8 Sue Shellenbarger, "When the Boss Is a Screamer," *Wall Street Journal*, August 15, 2012, accessed October 10, 2012. http://online.wsj.com/article/SB10000872396390444772404577589302193682244.html

Remember that your team members bring their own life experiences to the team and that your ability to terminate employment can produce fear in some people. The point here is that all of us can easily find ourselves relying on fear to motivate our teams – particularly when we're stressed.

It's not just "the other guy!"

 When you use fear to motivate your team, you ask them to give their least, or even worse, to fight back!

Chapter 4
Your Toolbox

"It is what we know already that often prevents us from learning."
~ Claude Bernard, Physiologist

"It is tempting, if the only tool you have is a hammer, to treat everything as if it were a nail."
~ Abraham Maslow, Psychologist

AT THIS POINT, you're probably nodding and recognizing how fear negatively impacts performance. Most of us can identify with the effects of fear and remember how we responded when a supervisor threatened us. We intuitively understand that fear makes us tight and keeps us from doing our best.

So why do we use fear as a management tool?

Why did Mikayla's manager rely on fear? Why did Kimberly's great leadership intentions fade away so quickly when she got her poor sales figures?

Before we explore the tools that will help us build engaged, committed, innovative teams, let's take a look at why we use fear. After all, if it's so common, fear must have something going for it, right?

There are three reasons leaders use fear:

1.   It's easy.
2.   It works.
3.   They lack other tools.

Let's briefly examine each of these.

FEAR IS EASY

Picture yourself sitting down at a dining room table to change the batteries in a child's toy. You flip the toy upside down and discover that a small screw fastens the panel you need to open to get at the batteries. On your table is a butter knife with a thin edge. Across the house, in your garage, is a small screwdriver that's just the right size for this screw.

Which tool would you use: the knife or the screwdriver?

Don't feel bad if you chose the knife – I've certainly unscrewed my fair share of screws using a knife.

If you chose the knife, you used it because it was easy. It was available and you could get the job done right away. The negative consequences of using the knife (blunted edge, stripped screws, and cutting your hand – all of which I've done) were of less concern than the ease of opening that battery compartment right away.

As a motivational tool, fear is a lot like that butter knife: easy, accessible, and less work right now than the alternatives. Fear is easy because it comes naturally and it's accessible because most of us learned it at an early age.

That fight or flight response comes naturally to all of us. While we like to think of ourselves as rational beings, the truth is that the more primitive and emotional parts of our brain act first and powerfully when we make decisions. [9]

Watch any advertising and you'll quickly see the dominant themes: wealth, power, security, status, fear, safety, and sex. These themes appeal

---

9 Pfister, H.R., & Böhm, G. "The multiplicity of emotions: A framework of emotional functions in decision making," *Judgment and decision making*, (2008): 3(1), 5-17.

to the emotional part of your brain. Then the advertisers follow up with something to help your intellect rationalize the purchase.

Even beyond our built-in survival instincts, as a child you likely learned how to use fear as a motivator. When my father instructed me to get the house clean, there was an implied "or else." I didn't know what it would be, but I didn't want to find out!

In the United States, there is a saying among so many mothers that it is nearly cliché: "I'm your mother – I brought you into this world and I can take you out!" While it's often said tongue-in-cheek, many children grow up understanding that failure to do what is required will result in harsh consequences. Moreover, far too many children grow up in homes where fear is more than just a constructive disciplinary tool, but a visceral part of a life spent trying to survive abusive or alcoholic parents.

Once you arrived at school or the playground, you likely encountered other children and teachers who relied on fear. Unfortunately, you can find bullies in the schoolyard *and* the classroom. By your teenage years, you likely encountered teachers and other children who relied on fear of punishment, fear of rejection, or fear of pain to get compliance.

I don't mean to judge these parents, teachers, and childhood peers for their use of fear. Too often, their own upbringing, insecurity, or sense of powerlessness caused them to use fear. That's not an excuse, but it is a reality.

The point is: we learn fear early in our lives. It is hardwired into our brains and reinforced from an early age.

No wonder it comes so easily to so many leaders.

FEAR WORKS

One of the most seductive characteristics of fear is that it does work – at least a little bit. Remember that robber in the parking lot? He did manage to get a few dollars. Relative to everything in your bank account, it may have been minimal, but he did get something.

Likewise, a teacher or manager who uses fear *can* get results. The results are limited, they don't tap into the power of deep motivations, and they are ultimately short-lived and even self-defeating, but for a moment, we have results.

Consequently, managers who are insecure and focused on the short term often rely on fear because they can get at least a little something done. Then they become frustrated, bitter, and disillusioned with people who only respond to fear.

They get caught in a vicious spiral where they get results from fear alone and then believe fear is the only way to get results. This spiral can last quite a while and some of these leaders may even get promoted.

At a minimal level, fear can get results.

LACK OF TOOLS

Remember that battery compartment?

What if there was a butter knife on the table in front of you and you didn't own a screwdriver?

In that case, you might use the knife simply because you didn't have any other tool available.

For some leaders, that's why they consistently rely on fear – it's all they know. Newer leaders, supervisors, and managers may not have learned anything else yet; veteran leaders may have used fear early in their career, fallen into a destructive spiral of fear, and slowly built a worldview where fear is all that works.

Regardless of how they got there, leaders who rely on fear to motivate their teams often do so because they lack other tools or don't know how to use other tools (and therefore believe those tools don't work).

A BETTER WAY

After 20 years of studying leadership, speaking about leadership, leading teams and companies, and more than 2000 sessions coaching leaders, I am more convinced than ever that there is a better way. You can get more done, increase employee engagement, and achieve results in whatever you do if you apply some basic principles of human influence.

These principles of influence are not difficult to understand and you will easily recognize them in your own life and in the lives of the leaders you will meet in these pages. As you complete a chapter, you can set the book down and immediately apply what you've read…and almost as immediately begin to see results in your team and yourself.

At this point, you may be asking, "If these principles work and are so simple and easy to use, why is it that they are so rare? How can employees be so disengaged if the answers are right in front of us?"

These are good questions. I hope they haunt anyone who cares about leadership, effectiveness, and humanity's future. Many of the answers come back to the reasons we rely on fear in the first place:

- It's easy;
- It works at a minimal level;
- It's the first (and often only) tool many leaders ever master.

There are additional structural and institutional reasons for lack of effective leadership: choosing the wrong people, rewarding the wrong things, and creating systems that work against leadership development.

All of these are reasons we see poor leadership, but they stem from a common underlying issue: we get distracted. Despite our best intentions, life has a way of distracting us from our objectives.

This isn't a new problem. Humans have been cooperating effectively for millennia and for thousands of years we've recorded what works, how we can best influence one another, and we've passed that wisdom on through sacred texts, through master to apprentice, through tribal circle to the young, through university to students, through books to readers, and recently through blogs, webinars, and e-readers.

The knowledge is there…but we get distracted.

WHAT'S A LEADER TO DO?

When I started to formulate *The Seven Things Your Team Needs to Hear You Say*, the most important criterion were that these tools help overcome the barriers that keep people from practicing effective leadership.

Valuable leadership tools must:

- Be easily understood, accessible, and available to leaders at any level of management and with any level of education.
- Work – the tools must produce results, be backed by research and supported by personal experience.
- Be practical and immediately useable.
- Be memorable.

The *Seven Things* meet these criteria: they are based in simple phrases you already know how to speak, they have been proven repeatedly through research and experience, they are practical, and we can easily remember them through stories of their use, misuse, and our own use.

After sharing these seven tools with thousands of leaders, I am certain that *The Seven Things Your Team Needs to Hear You Say* can help you to build teams that care while achieving measurable positive results.

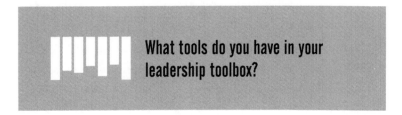

What tools do you have in your leadership toolbox?

Part Two:
The Seven Things
Your Team Needs to
Hear You Say

Chapter 5
You Can

"Everyone tells a story about themselves inside their own head.
Always. All the time. That story makes you what you are.
We build ourselves out of that story."

- Patrick Rothfuss, Author, The Name of the Wind

AS I WALKED INTO my office, my cell phone buzzed with a text message.

It was from Pami, one of my direct reports and a leader of two teams. The message was simple: "I want to resign."

We met for coffee that afternoon to discuss the situation. She looked up from her mug, her eyes watery, and said, "David, I don't think I can do this any more. I don't believe in myself."

Ouch.

That is a low feeling. One of your people...one of the team members you rely on, has lost faith in herself?

What made it worse was that *I completely believed in her.*

I had no doubt she was capable of doing the work and leading her teams. Something was missing between my belief in her and her lack of belief in herself.

I had failed to communicate the first thing your team needs to hear you say: "You can."

I believe it's a leader's job to be a C.B.O. That's: Chief Belief Officer.

In my early twenties, I had the honor to serve as an elected City Councilman in Glendale, Colorado. The Mayor at the time was a man named Joe Rice. Joe serves in the National Guard and has done several voluntary tours of duty in Iraq to assist with building local governments and civic institutions. After his term as Mayor, he went on to serve a number of terms in the Colorado state legislature and works today in the space exploration industry while continuing to serve in the Guard.

Joe's leadership success comes from a relentless optimism and belief in his team's ability to solve problems and get things done.

When we faced a contentious city government decision, there were often three or four opposing groups involved. The professional city staff with their interests, the elected officials (who rarely shared a unified opinion), service providers, and the public would frequently reach log-jams – even when everyone generally agreed that change was needed.

These three or four different groups would get stuck. "What are we going to do?" they would ask each other. Somebody would propose a solution, and it would get shot down: "Oh, we can't do that..." After a few minutes of this, Joe would say, "We can find 1000 reasons why this won't work. That's not the question. The question is, 'How *can* we get it done?'"

Joe's question presupposed that a solution was possible, and that we *could* accomplish our goals. Not surprisingly, we did. That one question and the belief it communicated was all we needed to break the impasse.

Walter Isaacson's biography popularized the idea of Steve Jobs' "reality distortion field." Although the "field" encompassed some unsavory characteristics (bending the truth, exaggerating, ignoring what Jobs did not want to deal with), it also included an almost magical ability to make the seemingly impossible happen. How did Jobs do this over and over again?

Issaacson relates the story of Jobs' visit with Corning Glass's CEO, Wendell Weeks, and how Gorilla Glass came to be used in the iPhone:[10]

> Jobs…said he wanted as much Gorilla Glass as Corning could make within six months. "We don't have the capacity," Weeks replied. "None of our plants make the glass now."
>
> "Don't be afraid," Jobs replied. This stunned Weeks, who was good-humored and confident but not used to Job's reality distortion field. He tried to explain that a false sense of confidence would not overcome engineering challenges, but that was a premise Jobs had repeatedly shown he didn't accept. He stared at Weeks unblinkingly. "Yes, you can do it," he said. "Get your mind around it. You can do it."
>
> As Weeks retold this story, he shook his head in astonishment. "We did it in under six months," he said. "We produced a glass that had never been made."

At his best, Steve Jobs had an unwavering vision of the future and a conviction of what people could do. He transferred that belief to Weeks with the simple words, "You can do it."

You can.

At a state correctional facility, Christine Aguilar had a problem. With no prior supervisory experience, as one of a small handful of female staff in a mostly male prison, and with a highly diverse and contentious inmate population, she had been placed in charge of creating a clothing factory. As if those weren't enough barriers, prior attempts to open a similar factory in other state facilities had failed.

Walter Isaacson, *Steve Jobs* (New York: Simon & Schuster, 2011). 471-472.

One year later, Christine's factory was out-producing the proto-type operation, had an impeccable safety record, and could run itself without supervision.

When I asked Christine what made such a rapid transition possible, she said,

> "It began with my belief in the people. When they came to me, they wanted to tell me about what they had done on the outside – why they were in prison. I cut them off, told them I didn't really care about who they were last year. 'This is who we are going to be in this factory and this is what we're going to do.' Most of them didn't believe it at first, but pretty quickly they responded to someone believing in them."

She described how male inmates would initially object to sewing because they thought it wasn't something men did. Christine would walk over to one of the industrial sewing machines, quietly operate it, produce a garment, return to the men and say, "You're telling me women can run this industrial machine better than you men? I don't believe that."

When Mayor Rice, Steve Jobs, or Christine told their teams, "You can!" their belief became their team's belief. Your belief in your team will become their confidence. Ultimately, this is the distilled essence of leadership: transferring the belief that together we can have a better tomorrow.

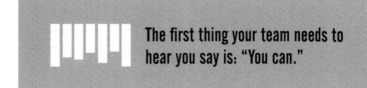

The first thing your team needs to hear you say is: "You can."

Chapter 6
Try It!

"Anyone who's never made a mistake has never tried anything new."
-Albert Einstein

A FEW MONTHS INTO her second year of college, our daughter Averie texted me with a question. In college and living independently for the first time, she told me she was baking macaroons for the student group she leads. She wanted to know what I thought would happen if she dipped the macaroons in caramel.

Now, I love macaroons and I've baked a few myself. I love them plain and I love them dipped in chocolate, but I've never had them dipped in caramel. I'd never even thought to try them with caramel. This is something I respect about Averie – she's creative and will try all sorts of things I wouldn't dream of – as long as I don't get in the way.

You see, when I read that question, my mind went into high gear thinking about similar combinations I'd had in the past. In a split-second, the chemistry of the Maillard reaction, the browning of the sugar in the coconut, the nature of caramel, the redundancy of the flavors, all went through my mind and, without ever having tried dipping macaroons in caramel myself, I arrived at the following conclusion: I didn't think it would work.

I started to type my response. "I don't –" my text message began.

Then I paused. I'd never actually tried it. Who was I to dampen her curiosity and the fun of discovery? Where would we be if budding chefs had never tried new combinations?

I typed in a final word: "…know," and hit send.

HELPING?

Many leaders and managers, in their desire to be helpful (or show off their vast knowledge) give quick answers when team members ponder "what-ifs." I've done this more times than I care to admit and I'd almost done it again when my daughter asked about those macaroons.

In my coaching practice, one complaint I frequently hear from leaders is that their teams won't problem solve on their own and lack creativity. Several issues can create a lack of problem solving and creativity, but one of the major problems is a culture that punishes innovation. New ideas have to fight through stifling layers of bureaucracy to be given a chance, or else the slightest "failures" are met with withering derision and criticism.

In either case, you will not see much innovation or creativity in that organization. It's just not worth it for employees to try.

The second thing your team needs to hear you say is the antidote to these innovation-crushing cultures: "Try it!"

"Try it!" is about making it safe for your team to experiment.

When you first meet Walter Rackowich, you might be surprised. As president of a Fortune 500 company, you could expect him to be gruff, busy, loud, or a dozen other Hollywood clichés. Instead, you meet a man who is soft-spoken, personable, and likes to laugh.

In November 2008, Walt became President and CEO for Prologis, one of the largest industrial real-estate companies in the world, operating in twenty-two countries with over $45 billion in assets. However, 2008 was a very difficult time to lead. In the elven months before Walt became President, Prologis stock declined 95 percent, and the company teetered on the edge of bankruptcy while suffering a major crisis in employee confidence.

Walt shared with me how he relied heavily on input and ideas from his team to address the crisis and try to save the company. In his words:

"Most of the solutions that you get will be because you've empowered others to come up with the solutions. Frankly, your people should be closer to the solutions than you should be. You don't need to be brilliant. You need to be a person that's willing to listen to other people, bring out the best in them, and foster great ideas."

As they worked their way through a massive organizational turnaround, Walt said he came up with only ten percent of the ideas Prologis eventually used.

When you act as if you must have all the answers, you prevent natural learning from taking place. Real learning grasps the essential elements, understands "what happens if," makes new connections, finds new solutions, and creates new visions. Be careful not to squelch creativity and risk-taking by trying to help when exploration is needed.

Rick Arthur is another leader who was given his position in very tough circumstances. He was made principal of Denver East High School in a midyear change, without any warning, when his predecessor was forced to resign. The school had been bleeding students and was under-enrolled by almost 50 percent. With no chance to build the infrastructure or team necessary to manage the complexities of a high school, Rick faced the further challenge that the outgoing administrator had erased all the hard drives and every computer file in the school's office.

If you'd been with me when I sat down to interview Rick about his experiences, you'd quickly appreciate his sense of humor, love of people, and encouraging demeanor. He shared how, in his first meetings with faculty and staff, he laid out the criteria what would govern their decisions going forward: attendance and achievement. "I made it clear that everything had to be about students being in class and succeeding in their education. That's what we'd been entrusted to do."

Then he encouraged ideas. "I told them that if it fulfilled the goals of attendance and achievement, then I was willing to try anything. As a leader, you want to encourage your people to get creative and come up with answers."

There probably aren't two institutions more dissimilar than an urban high school and a Fortune 500 real estate company, but Rick and Walt both faced significant leadership challenges, confronted organizations on the brink of disaster, and empowered their teams to come up with solutions. They were both willing to implement good ideas.

Encouraging your team to problem solve requires humility. As Walt put it, "That's the best leader. Not needing to be the guy with all the answers, but being the guy who can pull the orchestra together...and extract the best out of people." Interestingly, Rick also used the metaphor of a conductor to describe leadership. "You try to get the best from every person and make them the stars," he said.

SUCCESS TOGETHER

With Averie, I got lucky...this time. I did not rush in with my own opinion about caramel-dipped macaroons. Later that night, I asked how she liked them. She answered, "That didn't work out – I prefer them plain."

Nothing I could have said would be as poignant or as lasting. (But I still want to try one!)

During the recession in 2008-2011, I led a human service nonprofit organization. You would think the Great Recession would be a difficult time to do nonprofit work – and you would be right. Fundraising revenue contracted as the economy went into a tailspin.

However, during that same time we were able to almost double the number of clients we served. Like so many other contribution-dependent organizations, our funding dropped, but we were able to serve more young people.

How did we do it?

Well, it was not because of some great idea I had.

Two years prior to the recession, one of my team leaders, Manuel, came to my office and said, "David, my team and I have an idea..."

He explained it to me and I thought about it.

We had no infrastructure to support the concept. Making it work at scale would require additional staff training, investment in personnel, and resources. It was possible that pursuing the idea would be a distraction from core activities. However, it was very much aligned with our mission and it had the potential to serve many more young people in a way they needed.

What would you do?

As I thought about the project, I recalled one of my business mentors, Jim. He was from Iowa and never hurried. I'm not saying he was slow – he just never hurried anything. When it came to new ideas, he taught me the value of pilot projects. "Start small and try it," was his motto. As frustrating as that wisdom could be when I was in a hurry to implement my latest and greatest idea, Jim's advice proved valuable many times. Start small, learn from that experiment, and then try it again on a larger scale.

As I pondered the idea in front of me, Jim's voice came to mind. I called Manuel and authorized the project. "Let's try it! Start small – just one location. See how it works." Well, he and his team did. We learned some lessons from that one location. Then we rolled it out to several sites. We learned more lessons, then, just as the recession began, we rolled it out across the organization.

Manuel and his team ended up expanding our ability to reach clients during one of the toughest economic times that we've ever experienced.

"TRY IT" TIPS FOR SUCCESS

A healthy culture of creativity, innovation, and problem solving is not chaos.

To make "Try It!" work for you, try the following steps.

Provide context and clear criteria

When someone on your team has an idea, they likely are thinking only of what the world looks like from their perspective. You help them grow professionally and you make it more likely their idea can have meaningful impact when you share **context** and **clear criteria**. What is happening in the organization, the environment, or the industry that they need to be aware of? What are the boundaries within which they can play as they implement their idea?

Context

If you're a veteran and have seen your team member's "new idea" fail five different ways, instead of crushing the idea with, "We tried that and it didn't work," you can provide context for their idea.

You might say, "Well, tell me what you're thinking. We've tried some similar ideas in the past and here are some things I've seen happen with similar concepts. How would you solve those issues? How could you make it work?"

When you provide context, you give your team member the chance to problem solve at a deeper level. You're communicating value and respect for them and giving them a chance to grow. They might decide their idea won't work…or they just might solve a problem that's bedeviled you for years!

Criteria

When I think of problem-solving criteria, I'm reminded of a scene in the movie Apollo 13. If you've never seen the movie, it is the story of the Apollo 13 space flight in 1970. On their way to the moon, the astronauts on board realize their spacecraft is damaged. The rest of the story is the heroic effort to return them safely to Earth.

At one point in the journey, the air is becoming saturated with carbon dioxide and the astronauts have increasing trouble breathing. The only solution is to jury-rig a system that will clean the air for them.

The movie portrays this moment in a classic scene where one of the lead engineers on the ground assembles a team around a table. He gathers a box filled with materials the astronauts have on board and addresses his team. "We've got to make this…" he holds up a round filter, "fit into this…" he holds up a square filter, "using nothing but that…" he dumps the box of materials onto the table.

That is my favorite example of stating problem-solving criteria – fit this into that using nothing but those materials…and by the way, all this needs to be done in a couple of hours. This is what Principal Rick Arthur did when he said he would entertain any idea, so long as it accomplished the goals of increasing student attendance and achievement at East High School.

A final word about criteria – you might be concerned that boundaries can stifle creativity. However, the opposite is actually true. Clear boundaries and criteria aid creativity.

Here's a quick example. If I told you, "Write 5000 words. Go." You would probably struggle mightily figuring out what to write. The lack of criteria makes it difficult for your brain to problem solve. Now, how about if I said, "Write 5000 words describing your childhood until age 18 and using a popular movie from the last decade as an analogy for your life." Your mind would immediately latch on to the criteria and start problem solving. You might list a few candidate movies, then start a list of notable events in your childhood, and then look for similarities. Or maybe you'd just start writing.

Either way, it should be clear that criteria *enable* creativity.

REWARD FAILURE

This may sound strange, but let's think about the concept of rewarding failure for a moment.

If your people take a risk, but you only reward the risks that succeed, what will happen?

People will naturally stop taking risks.

By their very nature, *risks mean uncertainty of success.* By only rewarding the risks that work out as hoped, you communicate that you don't actually want creativity and innovation; you communicate that you're only interested in a "sure thing."

Avoiding loss is human nature. Most people in your organization will therefore choose to do nothing, rather than risk your censure for a creative idea that doesn't work.

The solution to this problem is to reward behaviors and attempts. Some organizations take this concept to a grand conclusion and annually give an award for "The best idea that didn't work." Others describe every new initiative as "an experiment" – a term that clearly communicates the desire to learn from the effort and acknowledges the reality that it may or may not work out as intended.

If you want people to be creative and innovate, you need to make it safe to experiment and take risks. When you celebrate creative behaviors, attempts, and even failures, you make it OK for the effort to not work and for everyone to learn something along the way.

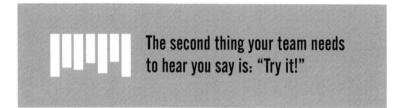

The second thing your team needs to hear you say is: "Try it!"

Chapter 7
I Believe

"A bird doesn't sing because it has an answer, it sings because it has a song."

~Maya Angelou

"A rock pile ceases to be a rock pile the moment a single mind contemplates it, bearing within him the image of a cathedral."

~Antoine de Saint-Exupery, Author, The Little Prince

WHEN I WAS SIXTEEN, I marched into the living room where my father was watching Star Trek, waited for a commercial, and then announced that from this night forward, I would be a vegetarian.

My father, a practicing vegetarian himself, said, "Great! I've got some articles on nutrition and recipes you can read later." Then the commercial ended and we watched the rest of the show.

After that night, I diligently watched my nutrition, I read the articles about amino acids, I learned new recipes, and I shared the dishes he prepared.

And I kept it up – for three whole days!

By day four, however, I'd given up and returned to my omnivorous ways.

You can imagine my reaction when our sixteen-year-old daughter, Averie, told my wife and I that she wanted to be a vegetarian. "You guys don't have to change anything," she said, "I'll try to eat less meat while I'm living with you and then, when I get to college, I'll be a strict vegetarian."

And she did.

During her final two years of high school she reduced her meat consumption and, since the day she set foot on her campus, never ate meat again. It's been years now and she's even taught me some delicious vegetarian recipes!

What was the difference between my daughter and myself? We both started with the desire to become vegetarians, but my effort lasted only three days, while hers has succeeded for years.

The answer to this question is one of the most important factors in leading an energized and productive team. Amazingly, doing this can easily double your team's productivity. What would it mean for your team and organization if every person contributed their best every day? What would it mean for you?

MOTIVATION

The difference between Averie and myself started with our motivation. We were both sixteen, but we had very different reasons for wanting to stop eating meat.

Since you know that my father was a vegetarian, you might guess that my motivation was to be like my dad…but you'd be wrong. That wasn't it at all.

In my case, like many teenagers, I just wanted to look good and get a date. In one of those weird, irrational parts of my adolescent male brain, that could happen if I only ate vegetables. That was my grand motivation and, as is often the case when our reasons for doing something don't make sense or don't go deep enough, I quit.

Fortunately, I'm old enough now to laugh (kindly) at myself back then.

In contrast, Averie's reasons were rooted in convictions that she did not want to contribute to animals suffering, that her lifestyle would be more environmentally friendly, and benefit her personal health and wellness. Her reasons went deep and she lived out those beliefs as soon as she could.

The difference between us comes down to motivation: her "why" was far more compelling than mine.

Now, this isn't a discussion on the merits of a vegetarian lifestyle. The point is that she had considered her "why" for several years, it made sense, and it was important enough to her to motivate her actions. My "why" was an impulsive decision, was ill-conceived, and didn't make sense. Consequently, it didn't change my behavior.

What does all this have to do with leadership?

Everything, if you want a motivated, engaged, and productive team. This kind of motivated engagement results from the third thing your team needs to hear you say:

"I believe…"

HOW TO BELIEVE

Have you ever caulked?

If you're not a handy-person, caulk comes in a big tube, which you then place in a caulking gun – a contraption that ratchets a plate at the base of the tube and squeezes the caulk out of the tube's nozzle. You use caulk to seal joints and keep them water- or airtight. For instance, you will often find caulk applied around windows or bathtubs.

If you're a professional or have a lot of experience caulking, you develop a good feel for how hard to squeeze the caulking gun and how fast to move the tube so that you apply a consistent bead of caulk with a minimum amount of waste, mess, and cleanup.

However, if you are a weekend warrior who caulks once very five years, you've probably caulked like I do. You get caught in awkward angles, constantly squeeze out too much or too little, and end up with a sticky mess that has to be redone. (And my wife wasn't too happy with the aesthetics either!)

One sunny morning in September, I was speaking to a group of sales professionals about building motivated teams. As is my habit, before the program started I was meeting audience members and learning about their work. Then I met Scott. He had invented a new type of nozzle for a caulking gun.

Rather than the straight, fixed nozzle you find on a standard caulking tube, his little nozzle had an angle to it and it swiveled. Scott was a laid-back guy, but as he demonstrated his angled, swiveling caulking tip and how it made caulking easier, his eyes lit up, he leaned forward, and he smiled.

Where did that energy come from?

It wasn't about the manipulation of plastic and sealant. His joy came from what it would do for people.

"I believe…" connects your values and heart to your team's work, by connecting their heart and passion to the work.

TOUCHY FEELY?

In my coaching and consulting work, I've met many leaders who lament, in one form or another:

"I wish the team was committed."

"They just don't seem to care."

"Why don't they take this seriously?"

Assuming these leaders don't have other dysfunctional practices, the missing ingredient in their teams is **heart.**

If you're an analytic or hard-driving results-oriented person, you might have read that last sentence and said, "Hold on now! Please don't start with the touchy-feely stuff. I'm responsible for getting things done and producing results."

And you are – achieving results is vital to your success. If your team isn't accomplishing anything, then there's no reason for it to exist.

That said, if you want maximum productivity, you want to tap into the most powerful driver of human effort…

The heart.

Every fundraiser and advertiser will tell you that humans make decisions first with emotion and then rationalize (or sometimes discard) those decisions with intellect. I like the way neuroscientist Donald Calne, author of *Within Reason: Rationality and Human Behavior*, says it: "Emotion leads to action while reason leads to conclusions."

Many nonprofit and service organizations prove this truth every day. They often work without the resources, equipment, and benefits taken for granted in other businesses and yet they persevere, working long hours, out of the limelight, and for less money.

Why? Because what they're doing is important – to them.

Your organization may not be a nonprofit, but the good news is that you can connect your team to the same source of motivation.

When you say, "I believe…" you express two critical ideas: Your **values** and a compelling **why**.

VALUES

Let's focus first on your own values and reason for being a part of the organization. A quick caveat: I'm not talking about the organizational values that were shared at a retreat last year or the ones on a poster or mug in your office. I'm talking about your personal values, your personal motivations.

It's essential that you are honest as you start with yourself. Take a moment to answer these questions:

- Why am **I** a part of the organization?
- Why do **I** lead?
- What values motivate **me** to do **this work**?

If you're confident in your answers to these questions, the next question is: Have you shared these reasons and values with your team?

I frequently encounter leaders who are struggling with disengaged teams who "just don't seem to care" and yet, the leader has never shared a single word about what motivates them with their own team.

The bottom line here is that if you want your teams' hearts and minds to be connected to their work, they've got to see yours.[11]

Go back for a moment to Scott, our caulk-tip creator. Imagine how he might answer those questions.

He might tell us about how he values a job well done, how solving a problem is satisfying, and how helping other people do good work makes him happy. He might say he's a part of his organization so that he can share his invention with others and make a living while helping them. He might tell us he is leading the team because he's committed to finding better ways to do our work.

Now imagine you work for Scott. He shared those values and motivations with you…when you interviewed, when you were hired, and at least once a month during a team meeting or again in individual conversations.

From the moment you met Scott to the moment you left his organization, you would consistently hear him say, "I believe in the value of a job well done, in making life easier for our customers, in solving small, but annoying problems. I'm here because those things matter to me."

It would be impossible to work for Scott and not know where he's coming from. You would know his heart and you'd have a personal connection to him and to the work. You might even begin to share some of those values.

That's when the fun begins.

---

11 For more on exploring and concisely articulating your personal leadership values and motivations, I recommend *One Piece of Paper* by Mike Figliuolo.

When you share your personal values and motivations, you are exposing your heart – and that invites your team members to connect with you and explore their hearts as well.

Over time, something interesting happens. You will draw to you team members who share compatible values and motivations. Those who are uncomfortable with your motivations will drift away and find other places to work.

Your team needs to hear you say, "I believe…these things matter."

When Rick Arthur took over as principal at East High, another challenge he faced was the school's negative culture. The school struggled with traditional urban education challenges: gangs, poor student performance, and declining enrollment. Despite these problems, Rick told me, "I believed that every single student can succeed if we expect success and I believed that schools must be a safe place to learn. That's why I was there: I wanted students to succeed." Rick shared his values every time he gathered with his team.

One of Walt Rackowich's values was humanity. Prologis manifested that value through corporate responsibility. In our interview he said, "I believed strongly that corporations must be active in their communities and constantly give back." Walt described how one-third of the time on corporate conference calls was dedicated to talking about what employees did throughout the world to give back to their communities. "In doing that, we elevated the sense of purpose that people had about themselves and about what was important to their employer. Being human was important to us."

COMPELLING WHY

Would you be interested in doubling your team's productivity by investing a few minutes each month?

I thought so!

In addition to sharing your heart with your team, you can significantly increase your team's engagement, motivation, and productivity by helping them answer one question.

This question is so vital, so full of life, energy, and potential that I can confidently say it is the most important question you can ever answer for your team.

Of all the fundamental questions, who, what, when, where, why, and how, the most essential leadership question is, "Why?"

This isn't a question about great metaphysical or philosophical dilemmas. It's about the most practical question every team member needs to be able to answer. Simply put: **Why** are they doing **what** they're doing?

Your job as a leader is to connect the "what" to the "why."

As a leader, when you don't connect the **what** to the **why**, you condemn your team to soulless drudgery. If you've ever seen the classic 1967 movie *Cool Hand Luke* where Paul Newman's character serves time in a prison chain gang, you'll remember the ditch scene. The jailers force Luke to repeatedly dig and refill the same ditch. The meaningless labor is designed to break his spirit.

Are any of your staff doing work disconnected from real meaning or purpose?

If so, there are only two possible reasons: (1) your staff don't understand the "why" behind the work, or (2) there is no legitimate "why." Unfortunately, as organizations grow, previously meaningful tasks can easily continue under the force of inertia and tradition. If left unchallenged, that inertia will eventually sap the life from your team.

When you say, "I believe this matters and here's why..." you provide clarity, hope, and purpose, but you also create an opportunity for your belief to be challenged. This is a good thing!

Every single task performed by every single member of your team should somehow serve the mission of your organization. If it does not, it needs to be challenged, reexamined, and a better way found... or the task should simply be eliminated. Otherwise, you've sentenced your team to do work meant to break their spirit!

2X PRODUCTIVITY

Connecting the **what** to the **why** is so powerful that you can double your team's productivity in as little as five minutes each month. I've conducted the below activity with leaders and team members in a wide variety of businesses and volunteer organizations and it never fails to leave people with renewed energy and a sense of purpose... and you can do it too.

At the beginning of a team meeting, schedule five minutes for this activity. Give people a half sheet of paper or index card and ask them to focus on a particular project they're working on. Set a timer for three minutes and ask them to fill the notecard with their answer to the following question: Why are you doing this?

Grammar doesn't matter, spelling doesn't count...just list as many reasons as you can as to why you are doing the project.

After three minutes, have everyone get into groups of three and share their answers for one minute. After one minute, have each group of three share their most compelling thought.

In just five minutes, you will discover a renewed sense of purpose, the business of day-to-day tasks is imbued with meaning, and people sit up taller, smile, and have pride in what they're doing. Frequently, participants in this activity even shed tears as they rediscover the meaning in their work.

Now, if you do this activity and it's obvious that no one has a clue why they're working on the project, then you know you have work to do. If that's you, don't panic – you've got lots of company. One study Stephen Covey cites in *The 8th Habit* found that just under two-thirds of employees surveyed did not have a clear sense of what their organization was doing and why they were doing it![12] They might as well have been digging a ditch and then filling it in again.

NERVOUS?

Does the idea of sharing your own beliefs about what you value, why you're doing this work, and why people are doing what they're doing make you nervous?

For many leaders, these are scary questions because some leaders may be uncomfortable with vulnerability, or they worry that they don't have good answers.

If you're concerned about sharing, being transparent, or vulnerable with your team, I understand. The first time you do it, you can feel like a new kid at school. Will they accept me? What if no one likes me? How will they respond?

These are tough emotions for someone in a positional leadership position to confront. What I can tell you is that if you'll take the risk and show up with your authentic self, you will be surprised at the results. I can also tell you that if you want your team's heart and soul engaged in the work, then this is non-negotiable. They have to see yours. Only heart connects to heart.

If vulnerability isn't an issue for you, but you're still uncomfortable sharing your "why" and asking "why?" for every task, you may be worried that you don't have good answers.

This is a good problem to have.

It means you're on the brink of a major leadership breakthrough. If you're unclear about your own values or your own "why," I strongly encourage you to spend time in reflection. Hire a coach, work with a mentor, or talk to trusted friends and colleagues. This is the most important internal leadership work you can do. Your leadership credibility and influence will skyrocket as you get clear about why you're doing what you're doing.

---

12 Stephen Covey, *The 8th Habit* (New York: Simon & Schuster, 2004).

If you don't like the answers you discover, that's okay. When you realize you're on a different road than the one you want, it's the first step to getting yourself on the right road.

TOUGH LOVE

Let me get a little more specific. If your "why" is all about you (e.g., "I'm doing this for more money, for more power, for more prestige"), you are right to be concerned. If that's your big "why," you have little chance to influence others and create a motivated team.

People aren't stupid.

If it's all about you, they'll know it, and you can expect them to do only what they have to do. Leaders who create motivated teams understand that people work best when their work has meaning (and your personal success isn't meaningful enough to them).

If you examine your big "why" and the answers sound shallow, vapid, and uninspiring, I applaud you for having the courage to go there. Now take the next step: Where *can* you find meaning? Why is the work important? How does it contribute to a bigger picture? And if you discover it does not…can you take steps to eliminate meaningless work?

One final thought: the more difficult the circumstances and decisions, the more important it becomes to communicate a clear and compelling "why." In the early days of the Prologis turnaround, Walt and his team determined that they would have to let go 30 percent of their staff. Walt describes this as one of the most difficult things he's ever done, but he did it by staying focused on the "why." He describes making the announcement to the company:

> We are going to lay off 30 percent of the employees because it's critical to the survival of the company and the 70 percent that are still going to work here. If we don't do this, nobody has a

job. Second thing is, know that we are going to treat every-body with incredible dignity and we will give you packages that we think you will find extremely fair.

In that one announcement Walt communicated a clear and compelling "why": to save the company and preserve 70 percent of the jobs. He also communicated his belief in treating people humanely.

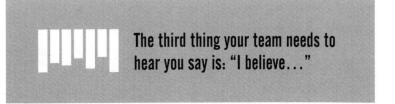

The third thing your team needs to hear you say is: "I believe…"

Chapter 8
How Can I Help?

"The true test of the effectiveness of the leader is this: Are your people better off when they leave than when they arrived?"
~James C. Hunter, Author, The World's Most
Powerful Leadership Principle

"DAVID, I JUST DON'T have time. There so much to do that some days I just want to give up!"

Lynn was a midlevel manager in a mid-sized healthcare company. She'd sought out coaching because the demands of her job were nearly unbearable. Between the needs of her team members and her supervisor's expectations, she'd been working 60-hour weeks, her health was suffering, and she'd reached the end of her rope.

Have you ever felt like Lynn?

As the Great Recession came to an end, many team leaders, managers, and midlevel managers found themselves with more to do and fewer team members to do it with. If you're feeling overwhelmed, you're not alone.

Or maybe you can empathize with Jack: "I feel like I have to do every-thing and my people won't take responsibility or solve problems. I've got enough of my own work to do – I can't do theirs too!"

Whether you've been in the same position as Lynn or Jack or just want to get more done, you'll find answers in the fourth thing your team needs to hear you say:

"How can I help?"

HAVE YOU LOST YOUR MIND?

When I was an overwhelmed manager and a mentor first suggested that I ask my team, "How can I help?" I thought she was nuts. I'm sure I looked at her with the same stare of incredulity my clients give me when I make the same suggestion today. When you can barely keep your head above water, the last thing you feel like doing is to go ask your team how you can help.

You're just asking for more work, right?

Actually, no.

This is a common misconception about what it really means to help your team. As a leader, you are in a unique position to help your team in specific ways that no one else can. However, this does not mean doing their work for them. What it does mean is to ensure your team has what they need to be effective, to remove obstacles to success, and to help them develop their own abilities to take respon-sibility and problem solve.

When you give your team the help they genuinely need, that only you can provide, two things happen. First, they become more productive, and second, you have more time for the work only you can do.

There are three specific areas to look for when you ask your team how you can help.

EQUIPMENT AND SKILLS

Sue was a fabulous person and wonderful team member. She was motivated, always thinking about how to improve her work, an outstanding goal-setter, just one of those employees you love.

One morning, we sat down together for a quarterly meeting. During these meetings with Sue I often took notes, just trying to keep up, as she covered all her projects, goals, and ideas. She appreciated a sounding board to process her ideas and determine which ones were worth pursuing. After we processed her projects and goals, I stood up to leave and said in passing, "You've got a good plan, anything else I can do to help?"

She thought for a minute and said, "I'm not a technology person, but my computer's a little slow."

"Why don't you show me?" I replied.

She walked me over to her computer and turned it on.

Twenty minutes later, it had finally come to life.

That computer wasn't just slow – it was glacial. You could have used a Gutenberg printing press faster than this thing. How embarrassing! One of my highly productive team members did not have the basic resources she needed to do her job well.

When you ask your team "How can I help?" be on the lookout for areas where they lack the resources they need to be effective. This may seem a bit simplistic, but its very simplicity makes it easy to overlook. Moreover, simple doesn't mean insignificant. In fact, the Gallup organization's long-running management research has found that, after knowing what's expected of you, having the materials you need to do your job well is a critical driver of employee engagement.[13]

Ideally, you ask these questions before bringing a person onto the team. What equipment and skills does this person require to do their job well? Then you build your orientation and onboarding processes the answers.

---

13 Marcus Buckingham and Curt Coffman, *First Break All the Rules: What the World's Greatest Managers Do Differently* (New York: Simon & Schuster, 1999).

If you have a good training process in place for every entry-level role in the organization, great! Now look at your promotion practices. Do you have a process in place to ensure that people receive the equipment and training they need as they assume more responsibilities? What about shifting job responsibilities?

In rapidly changing work environments, it is all too easy to assume people have what they need to do their job. Don't assume – ask! I shudder to think about how much time would have been lost and how many opportunities missed if Sue hadn't obtained a better computer.

Principal Rick Arthur shares one small, but meaningful change he made in his school.

> "We had old broken-down copiers that couldn't network with teachers' computers. In order to make copies, teachers had to come in very early or stay very late on their own time – and the machines were always breaking. It took forever and was a major frustration. The district had a policy about equipment purchases that wouldn't allow me to get a copier in the building for a very long time, if ever. So I pulled together discretionary funds from the vending machines and purchased a high capacity copier and dedicated a paraprofessional to make copies. It may seem like a small thing, but the teachers were so happy. It made life easier and they could focus more energy on students."

I appreciate Rick's comment: "it may seem like a small thing..." Frequently, the biggest frustrations for your staff *are* the smallest things. They're so frustrating precisely because they are small and readily solved – if someone (you!) will take responsibility.

Speaking of responsibility, here is one final thought regarding equipment and skills: this is *your* responsibility. Even if your company has a human resource department who manages onboarding and training processes, it is your responsibility to make sure every person on your team has the equipment and training to do their job. You don't always have to be the one to provide it, but you must be the one to ensure your people have it. In Rick's case, the school district had a process for equipment, but it would not have solved the problem and he chose to take responsibility for fixing the situation himself.

Never pass responsibility for essentials to someone else. Your success as a leader depends on it!

When you take an active interest in your team's training and equipment, you're telling them that you care, that you're invested in their success, while also making it clear that results matter.

OBSTACLES

You've surely realized by now that I'm not a big fan of power-based leadership. In general, I believe it is less effective at drawing out the best from your team. However, every tool has its uses and there *are* times you'll want to use directive, power-based leadership.

This is one of them.

The second area to listen for when you ask your team "How can I help?" includes red tape, bureaucratic nonsense, inter-departmental foot-dragging and all the other silly barriers they encounter inside your organization. Work is tough enough without those sorts of things dragging down your team's productivity.

When your team encounters these obstacles and they've done what they can to solve it themselves, it's time to pick up the phone or go have a visit with the people creating the barrier. Have a conversation where you judiciously use your position and influence to remove those barriers and cut through red tape.

Respect the dignity of the members of the other department, but be an advocate for your team, the organization, and your mission.

Your team will love you for it and you'll gain a reputation for results-oriented leadership, caring about your people, and commitment to the mission.

Yes, the other team might not be fond of you for disrupting their systems. That's okay if:

- You maintain your respect for the people. You may have heard the saying, "Be tough on issues, but soft on people." Assume the other department is trying to do their best and not being obstructionist just to be jerks.[14]
- The obstacles you address are genuinely bureaucratic, nonsensical barriers to success. Those need to be identified and eliminated and it's okay for someone to be disappointed about losing their unproductive pet procedure.

In contrast, sometimes you'll discover that the supposed obstacle is actually an important and vital process that also serves the organization, but in a different way. For example:

- Sales teams add feature requests while engineers try to complete a design.
- Fundraisers expose donors to services while program people try to focus on clients.
- Doctors and nurses provide compassionate patient care while administrators try to make sure everyone gets paid.

None of these examples are true barriers. They all include well-meaning people doing their best to carry out their responsibilities and serve the organization.

---

14 For an easy way to plan and hold your difficult feedback conversations check out Karin Hurt's video at https://www.youtube.com/watch?v=-Uol2inMsE0

In the above scenarios, you can best serve your team by getting both groups together and discussing how to serve the ultimate goals of the organization. (Yes, I'm simplifying here and assuming their managers will have the conversation. Life isn't always that simple, but you still serve your team by making the effort.)[15]

The bottom line is to serve your team by advocating for them and removing unnecessary barriers to their success.

THINKING AND PROBLEM SOLVING

Do you find yourself:

- Doing your team's thinking for them?
- Wishing they would solve problems on their own?
- So involved with their projects that you don't have time for your own work?

If so, this next section is for you. These feelings are signals that your team needs help to think and problem solve more, or more effectively. Other signals include team members repeatedly making the same errors or frequently saying "I don't know" when you ask about next steps. All of these are indications to look for when you ask your team "How can I help?"

HERO OR HARASSED?

Most managers respond to these signals one of two ways: they get upset or they dive in to "help" by offering solutions. Unfortunately, neither response gets you what you want: more time for your work and more responsibility from your team.

On the one hand, if you get upset and chastise your team for bothering you, they *will* stop bothering you. They'll also resent you and begin dragging their feet rather than solve problems that need attention. But

---

15 For more on building trust with peers and colleagues see our article at: https://letsgrowleaders.com/2015/08/12/how-do-i-get-my-peers-to-trust-me/

hey, they're not bothering you anymore, right?

On the other hand, if you play the hero and jump in with answers, the immediate problems get solved and work continues. But next time an issue comes up, your team still can't figure it out for themselves and, worse, you've now taught them that if things get difficult, you'll just figure it out for them. Yes, you're the hero, but say goodbye to your own productivity!

The help your team really needs is not chastisement or to solve problems for them. What they really need from you in these moments are your questions.

Questions?

Really?

Yes, questions.

THE POWER OF HEALTHY QUESTIONS

Asking good questions is critical to freeing up your own time and increasing your team's ability to think and problem solve on their own. In these situations, a good question or two can quickly move the conversation back to the employee owning the problem and analyzing potential solutions, but they do have to be *good* questions.

Stephen James was President of Biomagnetic Technologies, Inc., a company that specialized in brain imaging equipment. He has served on more than twenty Boards of Directors, and in an interview with me he said: "Good leaders coach their people. You have to be transparent, approachable, and direct in asking the questions that need to be asked."

In my experience poor questions look to place blame and dwell on failure. Examples of poor questions include:

- Who screwed up?
- Why did you do that?
- What were you thinking?

In contrast, healthy questions focus on learning and on the future to generate ideas and solutions. Examples include:

- What is your goal?
- What did you try?
- What happened?
- What would you do next time?
- Super-bonus question – keep reading to learn this powerful tool!

Let's see how these questions work in practice. First, it's critical that you've actually provided your staff the training and equipment they need to do their work well. We're assuming here that the person has everything they need to solve the problem, they just haven't got there yet and they've come to you for help. (Or you went to them because you were concerned.)

TRAIN THE BRAIN

One of your staff comes to you with a project that's behind schedule. They're frustrated and unsure how to proceed. You've handled these kinds of issues before and have a good idea about how to get it back on track. Rather than choose to be a hero or harassed, you use healthy questions.

> You: What's the situation and what's your goal?
> Employee: I'm four weeks behind schedule, but I want to get this in on time.
> You: That can be frustrating! What have you already tried?
> Employee: [Goes over what they've done.]
> You: What would you do next time?
> Employee: [Shares their thoughts.]
> You: Okay, it sounds like you learned [xyz]. Now, what are your thoughts about how to make up the time you've lost?

Employee: Well, I could try [a, b, or c].

You: What do you think would happen if you try [a, b, or c]?

Employee: [Shares their analysis of each option.]

You: [Provide missing data or criteria the employee might have missed.] Given what you've said and what I've shared, which option are you going to pursue?

Employee: I think I'll try [b].

You: It sounds like you've thought it through. How can I help?

Notice that you never jump in and give the employee a directive. As soon as you do that, you've taken away their chance to think through the problem and figure it out. In some ways the brain is like a muscle and, like any muscle, you can train it. Through your questions, you've helped the employee do their own analysis and arrive at a course of action. If they were missing critical information, you provided the data or criteria, but you still asked them to do the analysis.

Assuming that your staff have the basic skills, training, and materials they need to do their jobs, this conversation doesn't have to take more than a few minutes. For a complex project it might take the time required to drink a cup of coffee, but it shouldn't take much longer than that.

Now, you might be wondering what to do if the person replies to one of your questions with, "I don't know." Don't despair – it's time to use the **super-bonus question**. When a team member says, "I don't know," most managers will then jump in and supply the answer, but not you!

"I don't know" can mean many things. Rarely does it mean the person has zero thoughts about the issue. More often, "I don't know" translates to:

- "I'm uncertain."
- "I don't want to commit before I know where you stand."

- "I haven't thought about it yet."
- "I don't want to think about it."
- "Will you please just tell me what to do?"
- "I'm scared about getting it wrong."

What other phrases would you add to this list? There are many others because, when people say, "I don't know," they often use the phrase to cover another source of anxiety.

Your job as a leader is to continue the dialogue – to ease the person through their anxiety and train their brain to engage. This is where the **super-bonus question** comes in. With one question you can re-engage them in the conversation and move through "I don't know" to productivity.

When someone says, "I don't know," your **super-bonus question** is: "What might you do if you did know?"[16]

Before you judge this tool, try it.

Try it with your children, with your coworkers, or with the person next to you in a coffee shop. In any conversation where someone says, "I don't know," respond with a gentle, "What might you do if you did know?" and watch what happens.

It's like magic.

The person who was stymied two seconds ago will start to share ideas (usually good ones!), brainstorm solutions, and move on as if they were never stuck. It's amazing and hard to believe until you try it.

The **super-bonus question** works because it addresses the source of the person's "I don't know." If they were anxious or fearful, it takes the pressure off by creating a hypothetical situation: "If you did know…" Now they don't have to be certain or look for your approval and they become free to share whatever they might have been thinking.

---

16 I first learned about the super-bonus question from a colleague of mine, John Oliver. He was frustrated hearing "I don't know" from his employees and in his frustration he once responded, "What if you did know?" and, to his surprise, got an answer. I've refined the question into its current form.

If they hadn't thought about the issue or didn't want to think about it, you've lowered the perceived amount of thought-energy they must expend. You're not asking for a thesis on the subject, just a conversational "What might you do…"

Our brains can do amazing work when we remove the emotional blocks. When you do this for your team, you train their brain to engage, to push through their ordinary blocks, and increase their performance. Ultimately, they will be able to have these conversations with themselves and will only need to bring the very serious issues to you.

You'll know you're succeeding in asking healthy questions when a team member tells you: "I had a problem. I was going to come and talk it over with you, but then I thought, you're just going to ask me all these questions. So I asked myself all the questions instead and I figured it out."

Celebrate those moments and encourage them to start asking those questions of the people around them. You've just increased your team's capacity for problem solving, freed up time to focus on your work, and…you've built a leader!

Here is one final application for all of these questions. Use them for yourself. You can have these conversations in your own mind, with a mastermind group, or with a friend. I remember the first time I ever asked myself, "What might I do if I did know?" and worked through my own mental logjam.

It works.

CAVEATS

When you ask your team, "How can I help?" you give them the opportunity to grow, take more responsibility, and solve problems. However, there are some hazards along the way. Pay attention to these caveats and give your team the help it genuinely needs – and that only you can provide.

Culture, Not Cat Carrier

When we adopted our cat, Twinkie, the veterinarian told us to occasionally put her in the cat carrier for purposes other than going to the vet. The idea was to prevent a negative association.

However, we did not follow her advice, and now our cat hates that blue plastic kennel because the only time she gets put in the carrier is to go to the vet. And it's never pleasant at the vet.

In the same way, do not save "How can I help?" for times of crisis. You want to create a culture of support for your staff, a culture where they know they are expected to take responsibility and solve problems, and a culture where they will also get the help and support they need from you. If you only ask how you can help when things are going poorly, you associate your help with failure. You'll have missed the meaningful opportunities to help your team grow and become self-sufficient and they'll prefer you not be around because your presence is a sign of failure.

Create culture – not cat carriers.

Must Be Present to Win

I knew Gary wasn't happy.

Early in my career, during my first midlevel management position, one of my team leaders was clearly struggling – he looked frustrated, sounded frustrated, and it didn't take a genius to know something was bothering Gary.

So I asked if I could buy him lunch and hear what was on his mind.

As we ate, he shared his troubles: he'd been disrespected and abused by a senior manager, his team wasn't doing as well as he hoped, he wasn't sure the company's vision matched his own, and so on.

Gary appreciated my invitation to lunch and the opportunity to be heard, and as he started sharing his concerns, I decided to help.

He was only halfway through his first issue before I interrupted and offered solutions, tried to help him see the issue or person differently, or pointed out where he might be responsible.

Finally, he looked at me and said, "David! You asked me how I was feeling and what's bothering me…quit arguing. I'm just trying to answer your question."

With the tools you've received in this chapter, you can already see some of my mistakes. I was telling and problem solving for Gary, not asking healthy questions. But I had a deeper problem preventing me from giving Gary what he really needed. Gary needed help and so do your team members, but you won't be able to help them if you make the same critical leadership mistake I did.

I didn't keep my mouth shut long enough. I wasn't truly present with Gary – I had jumped ahead to my own responses.

We so often think of leadership and influence as talking. We see rousing speeches in movies, we remember key pieces of advice we've heard from our mentors, and we know we have something worthwhile to share. However, when we think of influence only in terms of what we say, we leave out the most important piece:

Listening.

A recent university study found that when it comes to influencing others, your listening skills outrank your verbal ability.[17] It makes sense: listening builds trust and helps you get the information you need to offer your conversation partner what *they* most need.

When it comes to helping someone, good intentions don't make the difference. Effective action, what you do that works, means everything. I'd intended to help, but in my youthful rush to show what I knew and be valuable, I'd missed the most important thing I could have done.

---

17 Daniel Ames, Joel Brockner, and Lily Benjamin, "Listening and interpersonal influence," *Journal of Research in Personality* 46 (2012): 345-349.

When you ask, "How can I help?" be sure to really listen. Here are a few tips to improve your listening skills.

Put down the phone

Seriously. Put it on silent, put it face down or stash it in a bag. Get rid of it.

You simply cannot give someone your full attention with the mental stimulation of email, voice messages, and texts. Put it away and focus on the person.

Eye contact

Don't be creepy, but maintain consistent eye contact. For that time, there is nothing else going on and no one else in the world, but the person you're talking to.

Offer empathy

Empathy communicates that you understand how the other person feels. You're not agreeing, sanctioning, promoting or anything else – just recognize the emotions.

Examples: "That must have been frustrating." "Sounds like you felt like no one else cared?" "That would be upsetting." "Wow – you must have been excited."

If they don't know that you connect, why should they listen to you?

Summarize

Before going any farther, take a moment to summarize what the other person has said. Use your own words and ask if you've got it right. If not, ask questions or encourage them to help you get it. The idea is that you are fully connecting with both their emotions and thoughts. Until you've done that, you haven't listened.

Ask permission

Once you've fully connected to the emotion and the thought, if you feel you have something helpful to add to the conversation, ask permission to share it. This is a huge integrity move and demonstrates tremendous respect for the other person.

It doesn't have to be complicated. Something like, "I appreciate you trusting me enough to share those things. Would you be interested in hearing ways you might address that or is it enough to get it off your chest?"

When you fully connect and have acknowledged the other person's dignity, then you're in a position to be truly helpful.

You must be present to win.

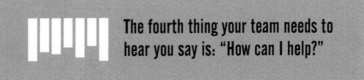

The fourth thing your team needs to hear you say is: "How can I help?"

Chapter 9
I'm Sorry

"We made too many wrong mistakes."

~ Yogi Berra

OUR TEAM OF TEACHERS and high school students had just finished a rafting trip, changed into fresh clothes, and loaded up our convoy of vans to head out to our hotel.

And I was leading.

I confidently led our convoy out of the parking lot and onto a frontage road that ran parallel to the highway before crossing over and merging – or so I thought.

With the other drivers in tight formation behind me, I led the team up a hill, but as I crested the hill and began descending the other side, it looked like the road was narrowing. I slowed a bit, but kept going – we were in the mountains after all and roads aren't always built perfectly.

However, as I continued down the hill, the asphalt narrowed until it was just wide enough for one vehicle…then it took a sharp right turn and disappeared out of sight under the highway. Then I saw it.

A round "cornering mirror" – the kind of mirror put on blind corners so bikes can see approaching bike traffic.

Yes, bike traffic…

I'd led my team down a bike path.

Now we were stuck – a line of vans pointed downhill on a narrow bike path. No room to turn around and no way to go forward.

Have you ever led your team down a dead-end? Your idea was ill-conceived, your information was wrong, or you just plain screwed up?

What did you do next?

We had to unload all the students and then slowly back each vehicle up the hill, then back down the other side until they reached the parking lot where they could turn around.

Also, I had to apologize.

One of my colleagues in particular found driving in the mountains stressful and my mistake only added to her discomfort.

I had no excuse – no sign told me to take that "road." It turned out I had misread a sign I did see and then trusted my own instincts.

The next words your team needs to hear you say will answer the most vital question they have about you: Can we really trust your leadership?

The times you screw up give you one of the greatest opportunities to answer this question. In these moments you have the chance to build your credibility and your team's trust…or to go the other direction and lose it.

The fifth thing your team needs to hear you say is, "I'm sorry."

Many times, leaders are reluctant to apologize because they fear they will be seen as incompetent or weak. This fear ignores one prominent fact: Your team already knows you're not perfect!

Just like my driving down a bike path was clearly evident to everyone on the rafting trip, your team usually knows or strongly suspects when you've screwed up.

It's not a secret.

Pretending they don't know insults their intelligence and makes you look insecure. Consequently, your team is unlikely to trust you. They're saying to themselves, "Gee, you can't even admit what we all can see," and they begin asking, **"Can we really trust your leadership?"**

When your team is asking that question, it destroys your credibility.

Walt Rackowich describes two benefits of vulnerability and the willingness to apologize:

> "Those leaders show an innate sense of humanity that people can connect with…people connect with that because they know they are not right all the time. If you never admit you're wrong, your employees won't apologize down the road either because *they* know they have to be right all the time."

When you refuse to acknowledge you goofed up, your team can't show up with their whole self. They can't bring the human part that makes mistakes and, because they know that's not real, they can't trust you either.

In contrast, when you screw up and admit it, own it, apologize, and make it right, you actually increase your team's trust in you. They know that:

- You are strong enough to do the right thing.
- You have integrity to admit truth even when it doesn't cast you in the best light.
- You do not consider yourself more valuable than your team.
- You are committed to solutions and the mission above appearances.

That knowledge adds up to suggest you're reliable, credible, and can be trusted.

When you make a mistake, there are just a few simple things to do:

- **Take responsibility.**
- **Apologize.** Use sincere, plain, straightforward language like you would with a friend or a spouse. Never apologize like a politician. "Honey, I am so, so sorry. I've got to take responsibility for that," (sincere, simple) is always better than "I regret if you felt bad about what I might have said." (indirect, political, blame-shifting)
- **Make it right.** If there is something you need to correct, fix, or restore – do it. Those vans had to be backed up and turned around. From a service perspective, sometimes it is useful to ask your team, "How can I make this right?" just as you would a customer who you've let down.

I've recalled that moment on the bike path many times through the years. When I make a mistake I know the shortest path to get things going right again is to "back up the van" and find the right road.

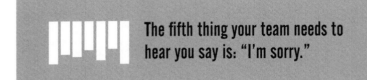

The fifth thing your team needs to hear you say is: "I'm sorry."

Chapter 10
That Will Not Happen Here

"It is the duty of the executive to remove ruthlessly anyone – and especially any manager – who consistently fails to perform with high distinction. To let such a man stay on corrupts the others. It is grossly unfair to the whole organization."

–Peter Drucker, Author and Consultant

WOULD YOU BE INTERESTED in a leadership practice that would improve the quality of work for 80 percent of your employees? What if you could increase the productivity and job satisfaction of 93 percent of your staff? What would that mean for your team and your organization?

Believe it or not, there is one thing you can say and do that can provide those benefits. If you've been in the workplace long, you will probably recognize this one quickly.

Many years ago, when I started my professional career, I came across a survey that asked, "If you got to be boss for a day, what one thing would you do?"

Before reading any further, take a moment to answer that question.

How would you have answered it differently at various times in your career?

You might expect the most common answer to be one of these:

- "Give everybody more vacation time," or
- "Give myself and other deserving folks a raise," or maybe even
- "Improve the quality of the food in the break room."

While those items were on the list, they were not the most common. The most frequent response was, "I would take care of the troublemakers and the people who are not doing their work."

In my own professional speaking I have asked this same question many times and, despite changes in the economy and workplace, the above continues to be a very common response.

In fact, 93 percent of employees report working with people who don't pull their weight. Underperforming coworkers cause one-fourth of employees to work four to six additional hours each week and 80 percent of employees report that picking up the slack for shirking coworkers lowers the quality of their own work.[18]

If you've ever worked alongside a slacking colleague, you know this reality firsthand. There's almost nothing more demotivating! It corrupts the soul when you have somebody who's not pulling their weight and not doing their job. For your highly productive team members, it begs the question, "Why bother?"

If you allow that situation to persist, soon the performance of your productive team members will suffer, or they will leave and find a team worthy of their skills.

The answer to the problem of troublemakers and underperforming team members is the sixth thing your team needs to hear you say: "That will not happen here."

---

18 Joseph Grenny, "Advancing Accountability in Your Organization," *T+D*, May 2013: 14.

You may voice this one with different words, but it is critical that you create a culture where everyone is expected to do what they need to do and to treat others with respect.

Every leader I've ever interviewed reaffirms this basic message. Walt Rackowich says part of being humane and honest is that when people aren't performing, you've got to tell them. "People need to know where they are and you can't string people out too long." Principal Rick Arthur emphasizes, "you aren't doing them a favor by staying quiet. You're actually hurting them."

Talking about what you won't tolerate says as much as what you encourage. Steve James said, "I always fired anyone I found discriminating. I was willing to be sued if that's what they wanted to do. But don't mess around with bad stuff. You must send very clear messages about what is unacceptable."

Once, after sharing *The Seven Things Your Team Needs to Hear You Say* with an energetic group of leaders, a woman named Mary approached me and said, "David, I used to earn six figures as a manager in a technology firm. I did everything on your list…"

I nodded and smiled until she said, "Everything, but number six."

"That is a hard one for many leaders," I replied.

"Yes, but it's also the reason I don't work there any more – they fired me because I didn't take care of those things. I had to learn that lesson the hard way. Make sure you emphasize this one!"

Mary wanted to be sure everyone understands that you can say all six of the other items on this list, but if you fail to say number six, your credibility and influence will inevitably suffer.

If you're a nonprofit leader or leader of volunteers, this applies every bit as much to you as it does a leader in a for-profit company – if not more so! Imagine a volunteer who contributes their time and energy, works diligently, and always strives to do their best, working alongside someone who is no more than half-hearted in their efforts.

What will happen to your hard-working volunteer?

The same thing that happens to a paid employee – they will lose heart and possibly leave altogether.

When you say, "That will not happen here," you provide safety and accountability. Teams need these things. In fact, after surveying tens of thousands of employees around the world, the Gallup organization cites safety as one of the four most critical things employees need from their leaders.[19]

When you hold people accountable for their work and behavior, you communicate that what they're doing matters. You demonstrate respect and value for your mission, for the work, and for your employees. Failing to practice accountability devalues the mission, the work, and disrespects your staff.

WHEN IT'S TIME TO SAY GOODBYE

Not everyone is meant to be a part of every team.

On the surface, this may seem self-evident and yet, you've probably been a part of an organization or team that suffered because those with the responsibility to ensure fit and mission alignment did not do their job.

If you lead, there will come a time when you realize a team member is no longer committed to the mission or is not, or never was, a good fit for the organization. In these situations you need to make sure that you've made reasonable efforts to help them (reinforce expectations, alert them to the issue, provide any needed training, if appropriate, and practice your company's due process), but if you've done this and it's clear that the person needs to move on, the most important thing you can do for your team, for your own credibility, and for the employee is to help them go.

Many leaders struggle with the decision to remove an employee from the team. This isn't necessarily a bad thing. When asked about firing an employee, Dick Saunders, who we'll get to know more in the next chap-

---

19 Tom Rath and Barry Conchie, *Strengths Based Leadership: Great Leaders, Teams, and Why People Follow* (New York: Gallup, 2009).

ter, said, "If you ever reach a place where you can affect a person's livelihood and family without a second thought, then it's time for you to resign." You should weigh the issues and make thoughtful decisions, but there will still be times when asking an employee to leave is necessary.

Christine Aguilar said part of the reason her clothing factory operated for so long without a single accident was due to her willingness to draw a line about who would be allowed to work there.

> "If I had anyone who refused to work, to treat the people around them fairly, or was unsafe, they were warned...and then I fired them. I didn't know if I had the authority to fire anyone or not, but I did. I sent them to work in the morgue. I only had to do it a few times and then everyone knew how things worked in our factory, no matter how it might be in the rest of the facility."

I opened this chapter with a portion of management expert Peter Drucker's thoughts on removing underperformers. He continues that thought with regard to underperforming managers:

> "It is grossly unfair to his subordinates who are deprived by their superior's inadequacy of opportunities for achievement and recognition. Above all, it is senseless cruelty to the man himself. He knows that he is inadequate whether he admits it to himself or not."

This is a vital part of knowing how to say goodbye – to realize that you do not do an employee any favor by tolerating poor performance, mission misalignment, or abuse of coworkers. In the case of mission misalignment, you are preventing the individual from learning more about his or her own strengths. In the instance of negligence or abuse, you enable poor behavior and prevent the individual from learning how to succeed in the real world.

In either case, while saying goodbye to employees is usually not pleasant or something you would look forward to, it can definitely be an act of caring if your motivations center on both what is best for the individual and what is best for the organization.

Great leaders know when and how to say goodbye because they recognize that in doing so they express value for their team, for the mission, and even for the departing staff member.

 The sixth thing your team needs to hear you say is: "That will not happen here."

Chapter 11
Nice!

"Our chief want is someone who will inspire us to be what we know we could be."

~Ralph Waldo Emerson

RICHARD SAUNDERS, who goes by "Dick" Saunders to anyone who knows him, is an unassuming man with a ready smile and twinkle in his eye. Dick is a role model in Colorado's philanthropic community, having been a source of leadership and financial resources for causes ranging from ballet to underprivileged youth. Today, you cannot drive from one end of Denver to the other without seeing a banner waving his name.

Like so many leaders, however, his journey did not start with great success. Dick was born in Massachusetts, but after a fractured marriage, his mother moved him and his three siblings to Philadelphia. Dick eventually made his way to Colorado to attend the University of Denver. After college he married and started a fledgling construction business. "It was just the two of us, my wife and I, in a very small office."

Forty-one years later, that two-person business grew to become a $420 million company employing over 500 people. Today, you cannot drive through Denver without seeing a Saunders Construction banner waving proudly on a new project.

When I asked Dick about his leadership recipe for building a successful company, he replied with one word: "Cheerleading."

"I'm a firm believer that if you put someone in a good environment and they enjoy what they're doing, and that they're contributing, their productivity is one-third greater than otherwise," Dick says.

Even as the company grew, Dick took a personal interest in every individual's work. "I spent quite a bit of time in the field, encouraging laborers, asking about their families, making personal contact and creating caring relationships. That's being a good person, but it's also good business."

The goal, as Dick related it, is to encourage people's strengths. "You want them to do their best and trust one another with their ideas. If two or three heads are good, then three or four are even better. As a leader," Dick said, "you've got to have humility to listen to others' expertise and to encourage strengths in others."

Dick Saunders is the embodiment of the seventh thing your team needs to hear you say.

However, unlike the first six, I'm not going to give you specific words for this one. Ultimately, it is *your words* that matter.

My word is "Nice!" Your word might be "outstanding," but regardless of what words you use, the seventh thing your team needs to hear is **encouragement**. It might simply be those two magic words, "Thank you."

I'm confident you've heard the importance of showing appreciation before. I had too…many times in fact, from a parent, trainer, facilitator, or a team member. Then, one day I came home to find my daughter sitting at our breakfast bar. She showed me a fabulous project she had completed.

She'd really done well.

I had one little idea that could take her accomplishment "to the next level" and so I said, "Wow honey, that's awesome! Hey, you know what you could do? What if you add this to it and then tweak that over there? Man, that will make it so cool!"

Instead of being motivated by my wonderful, inspiring, universe-changing idea, she frowned and said, "Why is nothing I do ever good enough?"

Ouch.

That moment so many years ago was a powerful time of growth for me.

Many leaders are motivated by a vision for how things can be better. It's a vital leadership ingredient, but there's a temptation that comes with that desire. I inflicted it upon my daughter – in my rush to move to tomorrow, I failed to appreciate today – or her.

Tomorrow is shiny, new, improved, and wonderful. Today is messy, complicated, and familiar. You can push so hard for tomorrow that you neglect today.

Ignoring today is a problem. Today is all you have – it's where you live and it's the only thing you can directly control. Pushing for tomorrow is necessary. It's part of communicating "You Can!" and "I Believe," but living life continually pushing for a better tomorrow can suck all the joy out of today and leave you bitter and frustrated – and that's no way to live.

If you are particularly susceptible to this temptation, be on the lookout for chances to embrace today. When someone (like your child or team member) shares an accomplishment:

- Celebrate with them.
- Ask them what they like most about their accomplishment, what the most challenging aspect was, what they are most proud of.
- Explore the positive consequences of what they've done.

- Offer to share their accomplishment with others (and respect their wishes either way).
- Smile. Clap. Cheer. Ring a bell. Whatever is sincere for you.
- Find what is right. Be on the lookout for good things today. You will find what you're looking for.

MEANINGFUL ENCOURAGEMENT

If you had been with me on Christmas morning, 1998, you would have seen my wife open a gift I was quite excited about. We were celebrating our first married Christmas together and I had put a fair amount of time into picking out a gift I thought would both surprise and delight her.

When we were married, she brought with her a little 10-gallon aquarium that had seen better days. The fish were too big, the glass was scratched, and the fixtures were old and faded. She had to put a lot of work into keeping it clean.

So for our first Christmas, I surprised her with a new, larger aquarium, complete with all the accoutrements.

Unfortunately, several hours after unwrapping her gift, I noticed she was down.

"Not what you were hoping for?" I asked.

"It's not that…it's just…I feel like you just gave me more work."

She felt bad about feeling bad and a few tears ensued. I'd made my wife cry for Christmas – and not in a good way!

I replied, "Oh, I'll be happy to take over the cleaning."

I really was happy to do it because (and here's the problem) I loved aquariums. I've kept fish most of my life. My gift was more relevant to me than it was to her. It didn't become a real gift until I added the maintenance. Then it became something she could appreciate visually while also enjoying less work.

My attempt at appreciation had almost met with disaster because I'd ignored some encouragement fundamentals. Encouraging your team and showing appreciation isn't difficult, but it will require you to be intentional. Here are three key fundamentals of excellent encouragement.

Encouragement is relevant to the recipient

My initial gift to my wife wasn't relevant to her. People receive appreciation and encouragement in different ways. Dick Saunders took the time to build real relationships with his team and to understand what motivated and encouraged them.

Some of the best leadership advice I ever received when I was a new manager involved learning how people liked to be appreciated. The advice is straightforward and you can do it right away. Ask them!

Some people like time off. Some people like a cup of coffee. Some people like a chocolate bar. Some people like public recognition. Some people hate public recognition. Are your employee appreciation gestures really just "more work?" If they are after-hours, for the younger generations, the answer is probably yes…but know your own people – ask!

Encouragement is authentic

Meaningful encouragement or appreciation begins with relevance to the recipient, but there's more to it than that. Meaningful encouragement is also authentic and valuable.

You communicate authenticity in several ways. First, be specific. For example: "I really appreciate you coming in early all last week. That extra time was the difference in our getting the project done," is far more powerful than, "Hey, great work last week."

Second, be accurate. Taking time to get your facts right communicates that you really do value the person's contribution. On the other hand, thanking someone for "their project leadership" when they served on a different project altogether comes across as condescending, sloppy, and insulting. (Yes, I've seen this happen!)

Finally, authentic encouragement is aligned with other organizational behaviors. For instance, it doesn't come across as authentic when you tell an employee, "You're amazing – I don't know what we would do around here without you!" at the same time as you give everyone on the team a raise – except for them. (Again, yes, I've seen this happen – more than once.) Make sure words and actions align with organizational behaviors.

At East High School, Rick Arthur celebrated success and encouraged his staff with activities that related directly to student achievement and school spirit.

> At every faculty meeting we shared something that was going well in their department and stories of student success. We posted the names of all the students going to college. I would acknowledge day-to-day success with branded mechanical pencils – small things that came to be prized for what they meant. I provided all the staff who attended cold football games with a letterman jacket – it reinforced school spirit, but also was a thank you for the time they put into the kids and the school.

In addition to authenticity, meaningful appreciation and encouragement is valuable. Value doesn't have to mean expensive. I knew a team leader who had a passion for Italian cooking. Once in a while, he would personally prepare an excellent meal for his team.

For his team, this was a sincere, valuable expression of his appreciation, but it's not something you could replicate (unless you happen to be an amazing Italian cook). It also didn't cost a fortune. It was authentic and it was valuable because of the personal time he put in and because it came from his heart.

Encouragement reinforces the right behaviors

Have you ever had a supervisor who congratulated you for doing something that you knew really wasn't praise-worthy, or worse, something you knew was actually detrimental to the organization?

I've seen many managers pile praise on an employee while the other team members rolled their eyes and said to themselves, "If you only knew…"

If your people work in teams, be sure to acknowledge the team as a whole. Singling out individuals for praise when they work as part of a team will backfire and encourage the very opposite of what you want. Wise leaders ensure that the encouragement and appreciation they show are for behaviors that contribute to the organization and team.

CELEBRATION

Before we look at how to implement these tools, I think it's important to look at results. It's one thing to share how Christine, Walt, Rick, and Dick led, but it's important to understand their outcomes. After all, you're leading your team in order to accomplish something and if you don't, there's no reason for your team to exist.

Christine Aguilar measured success by several criteria. "At the time, we had the most productive correctional-facility clothing factory of its kind. We even out-produced the prototype facility in Virginia." But even more meaningful to Christine was how her team operated.

> One time we had fifty percent of the population down with the flu, and they never missed their targets – because they didn't want to. They were proud of their work. Another time, I had to leave the facility for a few days. When I returned, before they knew I was there, I looked in and everyone was working, team leaders were managing things, and I knew we had built something special.

When Walt Rackowich was made president of Prologis, the company was nearly bankrupt. Three short years later, the company had recovered much of its value, shed its bad debt, and was the largest company of its type. Prologis was so successful that it became attractive to others and was able to merge with its next largest competitor. At the time I interviewed Walt, stock that was selling for $2.40 per share when he became president was valued at $41.50.

Dick Saunders encouraged and cheer-led his company to become a $420 million organization employing over 500 people when he retired. However, one of the most meaningful measures of success for Dick is that years after he retired, Saunders Construction continues to treat its people well and has maintained the management style he lived "through difficult times, new leaders, new CEOs, and a new chairman."

Rick Arthur described East High School's success in terms of attendance and achievement. "In three years we increased enrollment from 1200 to 2100 and had students coming from all over the city. We had a diverse school and were proud of it." Even more meaningful to Rick, however, was that every student had a chance to succeed and East High became one of the top 100 schools in the country for Advanced Placement test scores.

The seventh thing your team needs to hear you say is: "Nice!"
(With your words of appreciation, encouragement, and celebration.)

Part Three:
How to Say What Your Team Needs to Hear

Chapter 12
Into Practice

"Everyone who's taken a shower has an idea. It's the person who gets out of the shower, dries off and does something about it who makes a difference."

~Nolan Bushnell, Founder of Atari

HAVE YOU EVER FELT like you were being watched?

I had one of those moments as I stood in front of an automatic paper-towel dispenser. I was in the men's room at a higher end restaurant and I was waving my hands around in front of the towel machine, but no matter how much I danced around, it would not register my presence and give me a towel.

I turned around to find a boy on his tiptoes, washing his hands under the automatic faucet. He was probably about seven years old and he wasn't looking at his hands or the faucet. He was watching me. When he'd rinsed his hands he turned to face the malfunctioning paper towel machine and me. Then, with bone-deep world-weariness, he said, "It may look cool, but if it doesn't work..." and he shrugged his little shoulders and walked away.

How many books have you read and thought to yourself, "That makes so much sense – I've got to do that!" only to find the book six months later and realize you haven't put even one idea into practice? It happens all the time, but my hope for you is that you're able to immediately and consistently begin speaking the seven things your team needs to hear you say, to anchor them in your leadership tool-box, and enjoy the energy and results that come when you work with a positive, motivated, engaged team.

Here are a few thoughts to help you put these ideas into practice and overcome some of the obstacles you might experience. The first three times below address barriers you may face and how to over-come them. The second part of this chapter helps you get started on the path to lasting change in your leadership. (If you haven't already downloaded the free workbook, now is a good time! You'll find it at: https://letsgrowleaders.com/downloadable-resources/)

BARRIER: SASRNT SYNDROME

Does this sound familiar? You've just read a book – it's the best lead-ership development resource you've come across in years. The wis-dom smacks you right between the eyes and in your heart you know you are reading life-changing words.

Or: you hear a speaker present a powerful workshop and provide you with critical tools to expand your influence and engage your team.

Or: you come across a blog post – one of those cool lists that are full of practical advice so amazing that you feel lucky to be on the internet that day.

And then…it happens.

You fall into the trap.

It's a seductive trap and its siren song has snared many well-inten-tioned leaders. I know I've fallen for it more than once. The trap is problematic because it feels so good, but it's 100 percent effective at preventing your leadership growth.

What is this pernicious threat?

It's the SASRNT Syndrome. (I pronounce this as "sass-runt," but if you can come up with a better pronunciation, please email me!)

SASRNT stands for "So And So Really Needs This" and is the leading cause of lost leadership opportunities.

Here's how it works: you read this book, hear that presentation, or see that blog post, realize how meaningful the information is, and then, just when you might start to benefit from it...

You think, "So and so really needs to read this..."

SASRNT Syndrome can take different forms:

- "My boss needs to read this book right away!"
- "I just wish my manager was here."
- "My colleague needs this list."
- "I need to share this content with my team."
- "This is awesome, I'll share, +1, like, post, or pin it!"

SASRNT Syndrome describes our tendency to immediately apply a good idea to others before implementing it ourselves.

If you're a leader committed to the growth of your team, this tendency can feel very altruistic. After all, you're looking out for your team's interests and helping their professional development, right? Or, if your leaders frustrate you, it's very easy to sink into a whirlpool of wishing those leaders would practice what you've just discovered.

Either way, this seductive trap keeps you from the most important work: applying what you learned to you.

While I was working on this book, I checked into a Las Vegas hotel where I would speak the next day. As I unpacked, I discovered that I'd forgotten to replenish a few items including my toothbrush and razors.

Fortunately, the hotel was well stocked with free samples of everything I needed.

What do you think I did next?

Well, I did NOT call all my colleagues and the meeting planner to tell them how the front desk had everything they might need. Of course not. I picked up the phone, called the front desk, and five minutes later they brought the items to my room. I applied the information to myself first.

The next time you come across tools, tips, wisdom, and practices (including those in this book) and start to feel SASRNT singing in the background, take a moment and ask yourself a couple of questions:

- Is this information I have mastered in my own leadership?
- Can the person I want to share with look to me as an example?
- Have I committed to learn and apply the information in my life?

If the answer to any of these three questions is "no," then I recommend you do not share the information quite yet.

First, make a commitment to master the principles, practices, and tips you've come across. Apply them to your own life first and then invite others to join you on the journey.

If you skip this step and don't make the commitment, you will feel great – "Yay, I just passed on awesome material!" – but you will have missed a real opportunity to expand your own influence.

This is an essential leadership principle: take responsibility for yourself. Instead of starting with, "My boss is a jerk and she really needs to read this!" start with: "How can this book help me to be the leader I want my boss to be?"

BARRIER: FEAR AND ANXIETY

"But David, if I say that, I'll feel like a total hypocrite!"

Donna had come to me for leadership coaching because her team was not living up to her expectations and things looked like they would soon go from bad to worse. As she described the team and her interactions, I ultimately suggested that she practice the seventh thing your team needs to hear you say.

"Go around, find your team doing something well, and thank them for it, encourage them in what they're doing."

Her reply is one I've heard many times before from a wide variety of supervisors. "Come on, David, that's their job. They're getting paid for that!"

"I know, but they have a choice about how they do it, right?"

"I guess, but David, if I say that, I'll feel like a total hypocrite!"

I so appreciate Donna's honesty because she voiced a concern that many leaders have when they begin to practice these tools. They are concerned about being inauthentic, hypocritical, or even fear their own inability to perform the skill well.

This is no small matter.

If, as Donna was, you're most comfortable being very direct and giving little to no encouragement, expressing appreciation can feel very awkward and scary. You worry about being perceived as fake, but often, your concern is really nothing more than performance anxiety – can you really do this?

You may have the same concerns about saying "I'm sorry," "How can I help?" or "I believe…" Odds are, one or more of these are outside your comfort zone and you worry about how you'll come across.

That's okay.

You can succeed in saying what your team needs to hear, even if you haven't fully embraced the message or mastered the skill.

L. Hunter Lovins, an ardent environmentalist and co-founder of the California Conservation Project and the Rocky Mountain Institute, put it best. She said, "Hypocrisy is the first step to real change."

Lovins was responding to a question regarding "green washing" – the corporate practice of making environmentally friendly claims as a marketing tactic, rather than practicing a commitment to change. Her thinking is that when a company makes a marketing statement, they have at least taken one step…a step that consumers can hold them accountable for and one that opens the door to more steps in the future.

If you're concerned about inauthenticity, I think there's a parallel for you.

When you're willing to take that first step, to try even when you haven't entirely mastered the principle or don't feel it to the tips of your toes, you tap into a real source of change. If you're like most people, you don't like being a hypocrite. Taking that first step will lead you naturally to match your actions with your words.

This principle exists in many forms. You've probably heard "Fake it 'til you make it" or the coach's creed: "Act as if…" These are all the same idea – you have to start somewhere. I believe that starting with your words is one of the easiest places to begin (we all know how to talk) and has the added benefit of creating internal tension.

You'll naturally resolve that tension as you grow more comfortable and see results. And what's the alternative? If you wait for the skies to open, choirs to sing, and trees to burst into bloom as you fully embrace everything your team does before you finally say, "Thank you" – well, it will never happen!

Several years after Donna had sought out my advice, we happened to be at the same event. She found me from across the room and taught me one of the most important leadership lessons I've ever learned.

"David," she said, "I did what we talked about. I still don't know how it works or why, but things are different."

I didn't meet her team after that and I can only take her word about their change in performance. What I can tell you is that Donna was different. When we had talked about her team before, she frowned and scowled. Now, when she talked about her team, I saw a huge smile on her face. Her eyes even sparkled!

That's the power of taking a first step. Donna taught me that your words can change your team, but they will *definitely* change *you*.

BARRIER: HOSTILE LEADERSHIP

Another barrier you will likely encounter at some point in your career is a supervisor who wants you to do things differently. Perhaps they haven't yet learned that using fear and force get only the least effort from their people. Or maybe they do know it and they just don't care. Either way, you may have a leader who pushes you to abandon your values and lead differently.

This is one of those practical real-life issues that frontline and midlevel managers regularly confront. When you find yourself in this situation, here are a few tips.

Clarify the situation

- **Is the leader asking you to do something immoral or illegal?** If so, it's time for a full conversation about the issue. If they are unwilling to go there, you've got a tough decision to make. Depending on the situation and your organization, it may be time to talk with your HR department, with a supervisor further up, with a legal entity, or, it may be time to leave.
- **Is the leader asking you to stretch yourself?** If you're comfortable being an encourager and motivator, but your leader is asking you to be more directive, this might be a good learning opportunity. Look for the value and future applications of what they're asking you to do. Most leadership approaches have a time and place where they are most effective so take advantage of these moments to learn those tools.
- **Is the leader asking you to lead in a way that you believe is ineffective or at odds with your values?** In this case, continue on to:

Clarify objectives

In most of these situations, your leader is urging you to do what they believe is most effective. Rather than get into an argument about how to do it, focus on the outcomes. Ask what needs to happen as a result of the project or their suggested behavior. Be crystal clear about results and objectives. If possible, commit with 100 percent integrity to accomplishing those results. In many situations, this is all you'll need to do. You give your supervisor confidence that you'll accomplish what needs to be done and preserve your ability to do it in a way that is consistent with your values.

If you do all this and you still find yourself in a situation where you're being asked to do something that isn't immoral or illegal, but that disagrees with your values, proceed to:

Preserve Dignity

If you've never seen the movie *Glory*, I highly recommend it. Matthew Broderick plays Colonel Shaw, a white man placed in command of one of the first African-American regiments (including soldiers portrayed by Denzel Washington and Morgan Freeman) during the United States Civil War. Shaw tries to lead his men well, but encounters a corrupt General who orders him to have his men burn a town (an illegal order) or else have his men transferred out from under his leadership. It's a very tough decision and one that many frontline and midlevel managers can relate to.

It's a movie, yes (though based in history), but how Colonel Shaw responds in that situation taught me a principle that has carried me through many tough circumstances. Shaw decides to protect his men and gives the order to burn the town. Both Shaw and his men carry out the order with as much grace and dignity as they can muster given the situation.

No matter what happens, always treat your people with grace and dignity. No one can force you to do otherwise, even when you have to carry out an order you disagree with or when you're being treated poorly. Your team will understand and respect you all the more for having treated them well, even in a difficult situation.

WHERE TO BEGIN

As you read through the seven things your team needs to hear you say, you likely nodded enthusiastically at a few of them while some others made you wince. This is normal. All of us have natural leadership strengths and other areas that don't come as easily.

To begin, turn to the quick reference list of the phrases in the appendix at the end of this book or in your workbook (https://letsgrowleaders.com/downloadable-resources/), and next to each phrase, write an A, B, or C, according to how you currently use that phrase. be honest with yourself!

- **A**: I use this phrase consistently and my behaviors match what I say. My team would affirm both that I say it and live it.
- **B**: I use this phrase occasionally. My behaviors related to this phrase are inconsistent and my team would say I could say it and live it more often.
- **C**: I almost never use this phrase and my team might not be able to remember the last time they heard me say it or saw me live it.

When you finish putting a letter next to each item, look over the list. Did you have any A's? If so, congratulations! I've worked with leaders who honestly could not give themselves a single A.

The first thing to do is acknowledge what you're doing well and to keep doing it. This is the foundation you'll build on as you add the others.

Next, look over your B's and C's. There are two ways you can choose where to begin. One option is to focus on the "B" area where you can make the most progress in the shortest amount of time. For instance, if you feel strongly that your team is capable and you believe in them, but you just haven't been communicating it consistently, you might focus there.

The other option is to focus on the "C" area that will produce the greatest results. For instance, if you gave yourself a C in encouragement and your team has wandered for years in a desert without a single drop of praise or gratitude, you will likely see tremendous benefit if you start there. It will take more effort, but you'll get more return on that investment.

Once you've chosen a single phrase to work with, it's time to...

START SMALL

After missing my appointment the week before, I'd just finished a tough workout with my trainer. She'd made up for lost time and I ached everywhere. Afterward, I ran some errands and stopped into a cafe for a tea. I was exhausted as I stepped up to the counter and the barista asked me which flavor of tea I wanted.

I froze.

I drink tea all the time and I only really choose from two or three flavors. This wasn't a difficult decision, but in my exhausted state, I just could not form a coherent thought. The workout had not included any mental challenges – no logic puzzles or mathematical proofs – and yet, confronted by a choice between three things, I was momentarily paralyzed.

Why? Because decisions require energy and I had used up all of mine.

The same phenomenon short-circuits many good intentions. If you've ever made a significant lifestyle change, you probably did it in stages. Rather than taking up intense exercise and an extreme diet, for instance, you probably started by walking more, eating a salad instead of a hamburger, and then went from there. However, if you did try to change everything at once, you probably didn't succeed.

What happened to me in the teashop also happens to you anytime you try to make changes in your life. Decisions require energy. In fact, new research even suggests that in a single day you have a limited amount of decision-making energy.[20]

That's why you choose only one item from the list. If you try to simultaneously work on three or four, you will not succeed with any of them. There's nothing wrong with you, that's just how change works.

Now that you've chosen your one phrase, think about the smallest, easiest way you can possibly apply it. I want you to look for something so small and easy that you almost can't help but to do it.

For instance, if you chose #7 – "Nice!" what is the easiest way you could express your appreciation or celebrate your team's success? Perhaps for you, a written note is the easiest thing you can imagine. Great. Now what's the easiest step in writing that note?

How about taking out a piece of paper and a pen?

You're looking for the smallest first step you can possibly take – something so easy that you simply can't fail to do it.

Something like taking out a sheet of paper and a pen. That's about as easy as it gets, right?

The secret of small actions is that once you put yourself in motion, inertia tends to take over. After the paper is out, what's the next easiest thing you could do?

Write a name.

What then? Well, now you might as well finish it and tell them in a sentence or two what it is you appreciated.

If you struggle with procrastination or can't implement the things you learn from books, blogs, or conferences, commit yourself to one impossibly small step, and only that step. The small step will overcome your natural tendency to avoid discomfort or risk of failure.

After all, who can't pull out a piece of paper?

Your goal is to practice this phrase until it becomes an automatic

---

20 Roy F. Baumeister and John Tierney, *Willpower: Rediscovering the Greatest Human Strength* (New York: Penguin Group, 2011).

part of your leadership habits. Depending on which one you chose and how many opportunities you have to use it, this may take a month or even longer. Give it the time it needs and be gentle to yourself as you start to speak words neither you nor your team are accustomed to. Change takes time.

Now the good news: in less than one year you can fully incorporate all seven of these phrases into your leadership habits. When you reach a level where you can comfortably rank a phrase with an "A," choose another phrase, start small, and add it to your practices.

Just think about what that is going to mean for your team and your influence!

FOCUS

One blessing and curse of being human is that we forget. Ask any parent about the joys of parenthood and the blessing aspect of forget-fulness is easy to see. All the lost sleep, illnesses, and drama pale be-side the joy of watching your child grow.

The human tendency to forget is also a curse. As individuals, families, and countries, we repeat negative patterns, fail to apply the lessons we've learned, and easily forget values we believe in.

Part of this is in our biology. Our brains efficiently filter out background information that doesn't pose an immediate benefit or threat, and react quickly to all perceived threats. Our brains' first job is to keep us alive.

Succeeding as a leader will require you to do more than just stay alive. You must maintain your focus, commitment to values, and consistent behavior for very long periods of time and do so when it is uncomfortable, inconvenient, or unpopular. These things don't come naturally to most people.

The good news is that there are some straightforward steps you can take to accomplish meaningful change in your life. Begin by picking the **right problems, people,** and **place.**

PICK THE RIGHT PROBLEM

Remember the second part of saying "I Believe…"? You connected the "why" to the "what." Picking the right problem involves the same process applied to your situation. **Why** do you want to increase your influence? **What** will it mean for your effectiveness, for your career, for the world, for the people you lead?

Spend time to get as clear as you can about your "why." When things get difficult, your "why" may be all you have to power you through the challenges. By "pick the right problem," I mean that you can focus on the behavior (e.g., apologize) or you can focus on the reason why (e.g., to maintain my credibility and my team's trust). The **right problem** is the one related to your own compelling "why."

PICK THE RIGHT PEOPLE

Change may be difficult, but your brain has some important shortcuts that help determine your behavior. One of the most important change "shortcuts" is other people. When I worked with teenagers, we had a saying, "Show me your friends and I'll show you your future." Motivational speaker Jim Rohn said it in a more grown-up fashion: "You are the average of the five people you spend the most time with."

If you are serious about saying what your team needs to hear, one of the best things you can do for yourself is to surround yourself with other people who are on the same journey. Maybe you have a colleague or a friend in a similar position in a different company. Your relationships could be in an online or in-person leadership community, or you could work with a leadership coach.

Whatever route you choose, surrounding yourself with **people** who are on the same journey or who will encourage you, model for you, and hold you accountable is a useful way to ensure you stay focused.

PICK THE RIGHT PLACE

Have you ever struggled with making a positive change in your life even though you knew it was good for you?

I know I have. My struggle started when I dove for a volleyball and did not get back up.

I was twenty-four years old and I'd burst a disc in my lower back. The pain was excruciating. For months, I could not stand up straight or even sleep more than a few hours without strong painkillers. Ultimately, I had to have surgery to remove the broken disc.

After surgery the pain improved, but my muscles had atrophied, I had permanent nerve damage, and I could not straighten my right leg. I still remember that first walk around the block.

It was torture.

I had a long way to go if I was going to recover. I joined a gym and tried getting up early to get the exercise I needed before heading in to work. Despite having plenty of incentive to get better (after all I was still in my twenties and definitely wanted to hike, camp, and do all the things I used to enjoy), I frequently woke up at five in the morning to face the winter darkness, only to be overcome by self-pity. I hurt, it was dark and cold, and many days it was easier to reset the alarm and go back to sleep.

Then I discovered a principle that would change my life. Actually, there were two things I learned. First, I found that I had two people living in my head: Evening Me and Morning Me. You've already met Morning Me – sleepy, uninspired, self-pitying. Evening Me was optimistic, wanted to hit the gym, and knew I could get better with time and work.

Evening Me figured out the third source of meaningful change. One night before going to bed I picked out the clothes I would wear to work the next day and put them in my car, along with my dress shoes, towel, and soap. When Morning Me woke up the next morning, I was suddenly faced with a different environment. I could not get dressed for work without going out to the car. I couldn't even take a shower. By the time I got to the car, I'd faced the cold and dark and it was easy to just hop in and drive on to the gym.

Changing my environment made the difference.

Your environment is a powerful source of change for you. Just like your brain uses what other people do as a shortcut to determine what you will do, it also takes cues from your surroundings.

You encounter this principle every time you go to the grocery store. Think about a basic shopping list: bread, meat, milk, salt, vegetables and fruit. Now imagine walking into your local grocery store with that list. Picture the store and trace the path you need to take to pick up those five items. In most stores, picking up those five common items will require you to walk through the entire store, from one end to the other, with stops along the back wall and a center aisle.

And what happens as you cover all that ground? You walk past enticing displays that call your attention to upcoming holidays or the season. While you walk you hear music that has been chosen to put you in a buying state-of-mind. You might hear an announcement about fresh-from-the-oven bread available near checkout.

Then when you do checkout there are magazines offering to improve your sex life, weight loss, relationships, and turn you into a culinary wizard in just twenty minutes. If you have children, you're well aware of the candy placed exactly where kids have to stand and wait. It's all very intentional. The environment is created to maximize sales.

You can leverage the same power of place to support your efforts to change. There are many ways to do this and it's an opportunity to have some fun as you build your influence. For instance, when I worked on expressing gratitude, I practiced an old technique of putting five dry beans in my left pocket. Throughout the day I would transfer a bean from my left pocket to my right pocket every time I offered someone encouragement. The beans were an environmental cue reminding me to do something I wanted to do.

My wife and I celebrated our 15th anniversary with dinner at a fondue restaurant. For the dessert course they offer fruit that you dip in molten chocolate. Before dinner I went to the men's room to wash my hands (two men's room stories in one book – what can I say?). There was a poster on the door as you returned to the dining area that said simply, "Offer to share the last strawberry."

What a brilliant sign! The proprietors know that most of the people coming to their restaurant are there for special occasions, dates, or romantic evenings. This simple cue, placed in a location where it cannot be missed, increased the likelihood that even the more oblivious guys would end their meal with a selfless gesture. The couple would leave feeling good and associate feeling good with the restaurant. That's a great example of picking place – of creating surroundings that predetermine success.

How can you "pick your place" and create an environment that supports your use of the seven things your team needs to hear you say? I've shared several examples:

- Manipulate things you need that put you in a place of momentum (e.g., clothes in the car).
- Placing physical cues in your environment (e.g., beans in the pocket and grocery store layout).
- Written prompts (e.g., share the strawberry poster).

The possibilities are endless. If you like games, you can create a scorecard on your desk or computer and visibly record your progress. You can combine the power of people and place by committing to use a particular phrase with your team, using written prompts, and keeping score together.

What ideas do you have?

Our human tendency to forget, to lose focus, and be distracted by the business of life is a curse when it comes to creating meaningful change. Fortunately, when you know how your brain works, you can make choices that predetermine success.

Pick the right problem.
Pick the right people.
Pick the right place.

Chapter 13
A Message for Leaders

"As we express our gratitude, we must never forget that the highest appreciation is not to utter words, but to live by them."

~ John F. Kennedy

YOU CAN MAKE A DIFFERENCE. No matter your circumstances, your experience, or your challenges, you can lead a motivated, engaged, productive team. You can do this. I know you can.

Try it. Even if you're unsure, anxious, worried about what people will think, or are not sure your way of using a phrase is exactly right. Try it!

I believe *your leadership* is essential to *our future.* The world needs you – now more than ever. You will influence people that none of the leaders in this book will ever meet. I believe that the way you treat people on your team directly impacts the results you accomplish together. But I also believe, even more than your products or services, that what you do and say, and how you treat people, is the greatest legacy you leave behind.

How can I help? Life is a team effort. It would be my pleasure to help you think through questions or challenges you encounter. I'm committed to your leadership success. If you have a question, please don't hesitate to send me an email – if you have the question, someone else certainly does too. You can find me at:

- Email: david.dye@letsgrowleaders.com
- Website and Blog: https://LetsGrowLeaders.com
- Twitter: @davidmdye
- LinkedIn: http://linkedin.com/in/davidmdye
- Facebook: https://www.facebook.com/dmdye

I apologize in advance for any mistakes or inaccuracies you may find in this book. Despite a great team of editors and my best intentions, books are rarely perfect things. In appreciation for your willingness to make it better, if you are the first person to email me with a significant factual error, I will thank you with a virtual cup of coffee.

If you are inclined to use these phrases to criticize other leaders, please understand **that will not happen here**. Everything you've read is intended to help you maximize your influence, not self-righteously beat up other leaders. If you've made a personal commitment to use these phrases and draw out the best from your team, please graciously invite others to join you.

Nice! You have done something very few people do: you invested in your own success. You read all the way to the end of this book and have at least thought about how to use these phrases in your own leadership.

Thank you for everything you do for your team, for your organization, and for the larger world. Thank you for your commitment to treating those you lead with dignity and grace. Thank you for reading this book and thank you, in advance, for recommending it to others. I appreciate you!

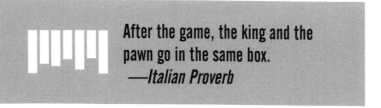

After the game, the king and the pawn go in the same box.
—*Italian Proverb*

Appendix:
Resources

The
SEVEN THINGS
Your Team Needs to Hear You Say

1. You Can.

2. Try It!

3. I Believe…
a. Share your values
b. Connect the "what"
   to the "why"

4. How Can I Help?

a. Provide equipment
   and skills
b. Remove Barriers
c. Ask Good Questions

5. I'm Sorry.

6. That Will Not Happen Here.

7. Nice!

Suggested Reading

If you are looking for excellent resources that can help you be a better leader and manager, I can personally recommend every book on this list.

- *Crucial Conversations*, Kerry Patterson, et al.
- *Death by Meeting*, Pat Lencioni
- *The Effective Executive*, Peter Drucker
- *First, Break All the Rules*, Buckingham and Coffman
- *Five Dysfunctions of a Team*, Pat Lencioni
- *Good to Great*, Jim Collins
- *Help Them Grow or Watch Them Go*, Beverly Kaye and Julie Winkle Giulioni
- *How to Choose the Right Person for the Right Job Every Time*, Lori Davila and Louise Kursmark
- *Influencer: The Power to Change Anything*, Kerry Patterson, et al.
- *Leaders Open Doors*, Bill Treasurer
- *Leadership and the One Minute Manager*, Ken Blanchard

- *The Leadership Challenge*, James M. Kouzes and Barry Z. Posner
- *Management*, Peter Drucker
- *Managers as Mentors*, Chip R. Bell and Marshall Goldsmith
- *One Piece of Paper*, Mike Figliuolo
- *The Outstanding Organization*, Karen Martin
- *The Oz Principle*, Roger Conners, Tom Smith, and Craig Hickman
- *The Question Behind the Question*, John Miller
- *Quiet Leadership*, David Rock
- *Strengths-Based Leadership*, Tom Rath and Barry Conchie
- *The World's Most Powerful Leadership Principle*, James C. Hunter
- *Your Brain at Work*, David Rock

Acknowledgements

Every river begins as a series of small drops, flowing creeks, and running tributaries that combine in a tumult of rushing water – and this book is no different. For your droplets, creeks, and tributaries of encouragement, motivation, and know-how, I want to thank:

Rick Arthur – A CBO if there ever was one.

Ed Tate – For sharing your journey and upsetting my apple cart just enough…

Darren LaCroix – For asking "how dare you not share…?"

Kevin Byerley and Glenna (then Gagliardi) – for sharing a meal and asking "what if?"

Manuel Aragon, John Oliver, and the many, many others who asked, "When are you going to write that book?"

Matthew Candelaria, PhD – for giving me permission to screw it up the first time.

Mary Kelly, PhD – for your generosity of time, technical know-how, and encouragement.

James Harman – for asking me to share.

Heather Lutze – for pointing the way, for locking yourself in a room to get your writing done, and your support.

Alexandra O'Connell – for your command of language, professionalism, and editing.

John Sellards – for layout and cover design.

Jan Dye – for wanting to know more.

Leslie Dye – for being okay with, "I'm writing…"

Averie Floyd – for teaching me, celebrating, and believing with me.

On Broadway and District 26 Toastmasters–for listening and making me better.

Daniel Bennett – for your wisdom and wanting me on the team when you're in the jungle.

Walt Rackowich, Dick Saunders, Christine Aguilar, and Steve James – for your commitment, for taking the journey, for your time, and wisdom.

Pami, Kimberly, Sue, and Donna – for allowing me to share your stories.

ABOUT THE AUTHOR

Author and international keynote speaker David Dye gives leaders the roadmap they need to transform results.

David works with leaders around the world who want to achieve breakthrough results without losing their soul (or mind) in the process.

He gets it because he's been there: a former executive and elected official, David has over two decades of experience leading teams, building organizations, and working with Boards of Directors to transform their effectiveness. He is the award-winning author of 3 books: *Winning Well: A Manager's Guide to Getting Results Without Losing Your Soul*, *The Seven Things Your Team Needs to Hear You Say*, and *Glowstone Peak* – a story for readers of all ages about courage, influence, and hope.

Known for his optimism, for making difficult concepts understandable, and for moving leaders to immediate, practical action.

David's keynotes and training programs help leaders across industries to increase their influence, solve common leadership frustrations, and improve productivity through practical leadership inspiration.

David has a BA in Political Science from the University of Colorado and a Masters Degree in Management from Regis University. He and his wife, Karin Hurt, are dedicated to their philanthropic initiative, Winning Wells, which provides clean water wells to communities struggling with access to safe water throughout Southeast Asia.

David lives outside of Washington, DC. He loves the meditation of a hiking trail, the reward of high mountain peaks, and is proud of the impact his children are having around the world.